transplantable organs, namely, hearts, livers, lungs and pancreas cannot be procured from living beings. As a result, most procurement of organs is from cadavers which is dependent on donations from relatives of the deceased.

Although there are stringent medical requirements concerning age, cause of death, health status etc. of the deceased to be fulfilled before a cadaveric organ is donated, yet there occur sufficient number of deaths under circumstances suitable for transplantation to satisfy the annual demand for transplantable organs. Most cadaveric organs for transplantation are those of persons declared dead by the cessation of their brain activity (or 'brain death' as it is medically known). On the basis of the data compiled by the National Center for Health Statistics in U.S. in 1996, Skumanich and Kintsfather concluded that roughly 7,000 - 11,000 people die each year from causes that would allow them to be donors. Since each cadaver is the source of multiple transplantable organs, they argue that the supply of donor organs could achieve a level that meets demand (1996; 401).

Thus, there is a vast discrepancy between the demand and supply of organs. On one hand, there is a large pool of patients desperately waiting for organs and on the other, there are sufficient potential donors to meet up the demand. Yet, these organs are not made available for transplantation. This discrepancy may be explained by the cultural opposition encountered by transplant technology in several societies and cultures. The reluctance in many people to donate or receive organs could be attributed to ethical issues concerning donation / acceptance, body integrity/personhood and understandings of life and death.

It is these socio-cultural issues that the book addresses and investigates across diverse societies and cultures by drawing upon journalistic, medical and sociological literature. The argument is that cultural perspectives often set constraints on social conditions which influence an individual's behaviour.

The success of organ transplantation as a medical therapy has raised several cultural and ethical questions about what constitutes an intact body. What is the symbolic significance of a body part? What constitutes life? How is death determined? What is significant to constitute a self or personhood? How is the giving and receiving of organs perceived? Should body parts be donated or given as a gift? Should they be treated like a commodity? What are the ethical considerations underlying these queries? How does the state respond to such an issue of organ commodification which is full of moral and cultural overtones.

Organ transplantation, thus, provides a fertile ground for exploring and understanding a vast number of sociological issues such as the concepts of gift and commodification, human rights and role of the state and its agencies, ethical issues of body, self, life and death.

This book addresses these issues and demonstrates how the medical technology of transplantation has made it possible to transgress and cross over the traditional boundaries of life and death, hitherto, considered to be divine creations. An effort has been made to understand socio-cultural responses, ethical perceptions and attitudes to the redefinition of concepts of life and death as propagated by the transplant ideology through an understanding of the cultural perspectives on transplantation of human organs. This book puts forth the argument that refusal to donate a body organ to a fellow human being which is considered unethical from the perspective of transplant professionals is actually a culturally conditioned response evoked by the process of unexpected cultural invasion by a new medical technology.

CONTENTS

1
INTRODUCTION

One of the distinguishing marks of modern science is the disappearance of sectarian loyalties ... Isolationism is over; we all depend upon and sustain each other.

- P.B. Medawar[1]

I

The present study addresses transplantation of human organs from the sociological perspective. It raises some fundamental sociological issues concerning life, death, body integrity as well as 'gift' giving and 'market' paradigms as ideological perspectives in the context of transplantation of human organs.

The study is inspired by a series of socio-cultural, ethical and legal questions triggered off by the success of clinical organ transplantation. As Veatch states, when Christian Barnard transplanted the first human heart, the first and most fundamental question that arose was whether it was unethical or immoral to take the heart out of a corpse of one person and sustaining the life of another with it (Veatch 1999; 201). Given the present medical status of organ transplantation as an advanced therapy, it is

1. Peter Medawar is the famous zoologist who provided the scientific base upon which modern transplantation biology is built (Silverstein 1989; 276).

interesting to note that ethical discussions in this field are fast outpacing the technological progress. The emerging ethical issues are wide ranging : Who constitutes a donor? Who constitutes a recipient? Why to give an organ? Why not to give an organ if it could save somebody's life? Why give it to strangers? Why give it to a relative? Who constitutes a relative? Who has the right to give? Who has the right to declare a person dead? Does brain death justify tampering with the body? Does a person who needs an organ in order to live have a moral claim to the organ of another person? Does organ transplantation disturb the natural and divine order of things? What is the religious significance of an intact body? Should men act for their own advantage? Should they act for social good? Answers to these questions are neither easy nor readily available. However, an attempt is made in this study to examine the answers that have been provided to these questions in the literature available for different societies.

II

Human organ transplantation began with a series of experimental studies early in the twentieth century (Karlberg and Schersten 1989; 228). According to Silverstein, among the many horrors that accompanied World War II was a marked increase in the numbers of burn victims seen in both military and civilian hospitals due to extensive bombings of cities. The sudden and rapid rise in the number of burn patients triggered off the possibility of skin autograft, that is, transplanting the skin of one part on to the burnt part within the same individual. Where the burnt area was extensive, it was realized that an adequate amount of skin might not be available. Thus, the possibility of skin homografting, that is, transplanting some amount of skin of one individual onto that of another individual, was explored by famous zoologist Peter Medawar who was assigned by the War Wounds Committee of the British Medical Research to explore this question in a clinical setting at the burns unit of the Glasgow Royal Infirmatory, Britain. He observed that the major problem that plagued the success of homografting, that is, skin grafting between different individuals was the rejection of the foreign component (that is grafted skin) in the recipient's body. On the basis of his study of the mutual exchange of grafts between a large number of donor-recipient pairs, he concluded that the homograft reaction is governed by the operation of atleast 7 antigens freely combined. This, according to Silverstein, paved the way for future research in organ transplantation (1989; 285-286).

Tracing the success of organ transplantation as a medical therapy, Gregory and Lonnquist inform that it was in 1954 when the first successful transplantation of kidney was reported. The recipient recovered completely and lived another eight years before dying of an unrelated cause. Following the success of kidney transplantation, bone marrow was first successfully transplanted in 1963 in Paris, the same year as the first liver transplant was performed in Denver. The first pancreas was transplanted in 1966 in Minneapolis. In 1967 Christian Barnard reported the first human heart transplantation in Capetown, South Africa. The first lung transplantation was performed in 1981 in Palo Alto, California (Gregory and Lonnquist 1996; 346). Since the first successful kidney transplant, according to Calne, was reported between genetically identical twins, its success was of limited practical value as very few renal failure patients had identical twins to provide donor kidneys. This must have prompted transplant specialists in Boston to direct their efforts towards performing biologically unrelated transplants (1971; ix-x). Over the years, the success of transplantation reached staggering heights due to rapid improvement in immunosuppressive drugs, surgical techniques, greater availability of organs, better provision for preservation of organs and care of the patients. Consequently, organ transplantation became a standard treatment for treating patients suffering from an irreversible organ failure.

Although transplantation has become a widely performed and standard medical therapy to treat organ failure patients worldwide, it has not generated the interest of sociologists and anthropologists to the same extent. This is evident from the limited availability of sociological and anthropological literature on organ transplantation. As Sharp states, "There is unfortunately a paucity of anthropological discussions on the cultural ramifications of transplantation in North America and only a few authors have conducted ethnographic research" (1995; 360). Similarly Fox and Swazey (in Gregory and Lonnquist 1996; 350) argue that the medical community became so overwhelmed by the cases of technological success in organ transplantation that they failed to consider the socio-cultural dimensions of organ donation and receipt processes. The focus of attention became so fixed on the medical success that the human and ethical discussions of the process seemed inconsequential (Gregory and Lonnquist 1996; 350).

With the growing success of transplant operations, there came to exist a large number persons who were eligible for an organ transplant but who had to wait for a suitable donor. As Dechesser noted, "Despite major advances in organ transplantation technology, approximately one third of patients accepted for transplantation die while awaiting a matched donor" (1986; 547). Dechesser also informs that the shortage occurs despite the fact that several people die each year under circumstances suitable for transplantation to satisfy the annual demand for transplantable organs (1986; 547). Therefore, there is an urgent need to investigate into the discrepancy between demand and supply of organs for transplantation. The present study addresses this discrepancy from a sociological perspective.

Although scientific and medical problems related to organ transplantation have been solved to a considerable extent, several questions have arisen about the ethical and moral relevance of the procedures involved. It could well be argued that these issues are an important factor that hinders the supply of organs, thus, posing a serious threat to the continuation and development of organ transplantation techniques. Daar and Marshall state some of these issues as those related to human rights, ethical questions involving the human body and the protection of its integrity, the meaning and realities of organ donation and the medical issue of 'brain death' that can only be discussed when cultural contexts are evoked (1998; 124).

Daar and Marshall argue that culture plays an important role in the perception of illness, response to treatment and the organization of medical care. In transplantation, cultural considerations arise in relation to the acceptance of this mode of therapy, the ethical issues associated with consent to donation and the social organization of the transplant program. According to them, cultural issues also arise in relation to the effect of illness on family, work, income and leisure and the side effects of immuno suppressive medication. They argue that the symbolism and beliefs attached to various organs, especially the heart, as well as the cultural conceptions of life and death and ideas about the body and its parts can be strong influences in hindering or facilitating the development of organ transplantation. Societies have various reasons, including cultural ones, for not accepting the new medical criteria of defining death (brain death) for organ removal. The cultural aspects of organ transplantation, therefore, provide rich material for understanding the beliefs and values that hinder the acceptance of organ transplantation. Such an understanding would, inturn, enable the medical scientists to adjust to them and introduce transplantation therapy to the people in a culturally acceptable framework (1998; 131-132).

A number of case histories cited by Daar and Marshall illustrate the interplay between medical transplantation and culture. For example, in Africa, a young girl was successfully given a liver transplant. Her health was restored and she gained weight but developed some of the body-image changing complications of immunosuppressive medication such as a round face and excess hair. Her friends thought she had become a witch and they ostracized her. She stopped taking the drugs. As a result, her body rejected the transplanted liver and she died (1998; 124).

Similarly, a young boy in Canada developed an end stage liver disease. His educated mother found out all she could about liver transplantation and decided not to subject her son to the procedure because she felt that this would violate his spirituality. The authorities wanting to protect the child took her to court but the lady won the case and soon after the boy died peacefully (Daar and Marshall 1998; 124).

In another case cited by Daar and Marshall, an American woman visiting Gautemala stopped on the street to talk to some children unaware of the strong belief held locally that missing children were kidnapped and their organs used by Americans for transplantation. She was immediately surrounded by a crowd which proceeded to beat her up badly and she became unconscious and ended up in an intensive care unit (1998; 124).

Furthermore, a member of the white racist organization - Ku Klux Klan was offered for transplantation the kidney of a deceased African American. When his health was restored, he felt so transformed in favour of the blacks that he went on to become an activist for the National Association for the Advancement of Colored People (Daar and Marshall 1998; 124).

Daar and Marshall show that in Singapore, like everywhere else in the world, there is a shortage of organs. However, the Human Organs Transplant Act of Singapore authorizes the removal of organs from a brain dead person unless that person has expressed an objection to this procedure. Since Singapore Muslims object to it, they are specifically excluded from the purview of this Act. As a result, the availability of organs is very rare in Singapore. Similarly, in Belgium, the authors point out how some of the orthodox Jews registered their objection to the concept of 'brain death' in large numbers and have therefore not become donors (1998; 125).

Maoris in New Zealand and aboriginees in Australia, according to Daar and Marshall, have very high rates of end stage renal failure and are over represented on waiting lists. Yet, their cultures do not allow them to donate organs after death. Therefore, they receive organs but do not donate which is strongly resented by others (1998; 125).

These examples discussed by Daar and Marshall highlight several dimensions of cultural perspectives on transplantation of human organs. An effort has been made in the following chapters to touch on some of these issues.

III

Organ transplantation has long been recognized as a miraculous procedure through which parts from one individual are used to replace dysfunctional ones in others (Sharp 1995; 357). The list of transplantable organs and tissues, according to Stickel, includes blood, cornea of the eye, kidney, skin, bone marrow, liver, lung, heart, intestine, pancreas, endocrine glands, ovary, bone, arteries and veins (1967; 37).

In the context of blood donation, Richard Titmuss raised the ethical debate over voluntary versus commercial blood in 1970. He examined such issues and questions as : Is blood a consumption good indistinguishable from other goods and services in the private economic market? If blood is morally sanctioned as something to be bought and sold, what ultimately is the justification for not promoting individualistic private markets in blood? The debate was then taken over and discussed by a variety of scholars such as Lightman (1982) and Schubert (1994). Schubert examined the incentives for voluntary blood donation in Britain, France and Japan. He observed that voluntary donor in these countries gives blood in response to some social pressure, e.g., in times of war when blood donation is regarded to be a matter of natural duty. Thus, World War II stimulated voluntary blood donations in western countries for many years. According to him, a donor may also give blood to a family member because giving is seen as a matter of family solidarity (1994; 204). Thus, socio-cultural issues related to blood donation such as blood donor motivations have been examined by several researchers. It would be interesting to examine the ethical and socio-cultural issues in the context of organ transplantation.

According to Sharp, transplantable organs fall into two categories. The first are the 'quality of life' organs, which include the kidney and pancreas. The second are the 'life saving organs', including the heart, lungs and liver. Organs of the latter type differ from the former ones by virtue of the fact that patients who need 'life saving organs' are in such ill health that they will soon die if they do not receive replacement organs (Sharp 1995; 363). Likewise, Sharp categorizes donors according to the type of organs. Whereas kidneys may be acquired from 'living donors', the majority of donors for other organs are brain dead or clinically dead persons who are maintained on respirators until the next of kin give permission to remove their organs. As such, living humans can only be donors of one of a pair of vital organs, that is, the kidneys or part of an organ such as liver. Since grafting organs obtained from the dead does not hurt the donor, it seems to be the most suitable donor source at present from the point of view of the transplant surgeon (1995; 363).

Human cadaveric organ donation for use in transplant surgery has, however, long been a controversial social issue. The controversy surrounds the ethical use of cadaver organs as well as the criterion for declaring brain or clinical death necessitated by transplant surgery. How is the medical concept of 'brain death' perceived and interpreted in a culture? For instance, in Japan, the pre-existing cultural definition of death is totally alien to the concept of death determined by the cessation of brain activity. What should the transplant surgeons do when a patient's brain has stopped functioning but his/her relatives insist that the person is still alive? How should the new definition of death be transmitted and explained? Should it replace the pre-existing definitions of death? How should the conflict between scientific medical norms on the one hand and religious beliefs on the other be managed and resolved in a particular society?

Gabr argues that "most people both in the developing as well as the developed nations are strong believers in fate and destiny. Although all religions express concern for the welfare of mankind, some groups argue that organ transplantation is 'an artificial prolongation of life' and therefore against the will of God. Some others such as Japanese, Chinese and Germans argue further that the human body belongs to God and thus no person, whether alive or dead, has the right to donate a part of it to someone else" (1998; 120). Such beliefs prevent people from donating organs. These observations should induce the sociologist to identify the cultural issues and perspectives that prevent cadaver organ donations. How do they conflict with modern, scientific and rational conceptions of body and its parts? How can a consensus be achieved, if at all it can be, between scientific and religious notions of life and death? Is it possible to transgress cultural boundaries in order to implement a medical therapy? How can the process of organ donation be culturally legitimized? These issues have been taken up and discussed at length in chapter 2, where it is examined and illustrated how the conceptions of death and the human body that accompany transplantation still provide substantial cultural resistance. The issue of organ shortage due to cultural resistance provides the focus for this chapter.

It should, however, be remembered that culture does not

always negate the concept and possibility of organ transplantation. There are enormous cultural differences not just between but also within societies. Therefore, no broad generalisations are possible. Gabr states that "a few religious leaders worldwide do accept organ transplantation as a means of saving life. Muslim leaders quote the passage in Koran which says that the merit of saving one person's life is equal to that of saving the life of all people" (1998; 120). On the basis of such arguments, it can be argued that resistance to organ transplantation is only one aspect of cultural ideology, the other aspect being its support and motivation.

Thus, another important dimension relates to the ideological supports for organ donation. How should the exchange of organs be treated by the society which, on the one hand are the private property of the individual and on the other, serve a social purpose of saving a life. Should humanitarian obligations be the primary concern or commoditization and profit? Is there an obligation behind a gift? Can organs be treated like any other consumption good? What are the consequences of treating human organs as commercial commodities? How are individuals encouraged to give their organs to unknown strangers from diverse cultural backgrounds? Should they be encouraged to donate organs or feel free to sell them. These questions will be taken up for discussion in chapter 3. The ideological controversy over organ procurement for transplantation provides the focus for this chapter. According to Joralemon, "the arguments about organ procurement reveal a continuing debate within the transplant community about which ideological alternative, that is, gift giving or property rights, will serve best as a 'cultural suppressant'. In both cases, the transplant advocates make use of the culturally familiar concepts to legitimize the medically accepted concept of organ donation" (1995; 342). Titmuss argues that "the ideological battle over organ procurement has created a moral conflict in the society by providing and extending opportunities for altruism in opposition to the possessive egoism of the market place" (1970; 13). Such a controversy between altruism and commodification ideologies will be discussed in Chapter 3.

In Chapter 4, we examine how the moral conflict between gift and market paradigms, between financial incentives and altruism has implications far beyond the medico-social domain extending into the realm of legislation on organ transplantation. As Titmuss argues "...Social policy, in one of its potential roles, can help to actualize the social and moral potentialities of all citizens" (1970; 238). Machado also argues that law operates as a symbol for what is regarded as natural and objective truth. It functions as a powerful normative guideline in defining and constructing social reality. In this respect, according to him, transplant legislation is particularly significant because in regulating the uses of human organs, it outlines the general relationship between the individual and society. This relationship is expressed in terms of the boundaries between the status of the living and the dead, mentally capable and incapable persons and in the rules for transfer of body parts. For example, the regulation of a social act such as that of giving or donating, points to the role of law in shaping what forms of giving are to be socially and culturally permissible, prescribed or forbidden (1996; 159).

In Chapter 4, we take up for discussion, questions such as what type of giving (donating) of organs is recognized by the state? What is the implication of a cultural controversy between altruism and market forces for a social policy such as the transplant legislation? Should the state regulate the relationship between donor and recipient, if so, how? Is legalising 'brain death' the precondition towards launching a cadaveric transplant program? Do commercial considerations always come in the picture? Has corruption crept into such dealings, if so how can it be eliminated? How is the priority to be determined - the individual over society or vice versa?

It would be interesting to study the motivation behind the transplant legislations in different countries. What is the impact which the transplant legislation is likely to have on the lives of people for whom it is framed? Does empirical evidence suggest that such enactments serve their purpose, if not, then why? Does the transplant legislation across nations display uniformity? Given the vast differences in conditions prevailing between different countries, specially between the developed and developing nations, is it possible to obtain such uniformity? What are the issues in transplant legislations which need to be addressed the most and can the enactments be improved so that the main problems in this area are tackled? These questions are discussed in the course of chapter 4. The chapter focusses on transplant Acts across nations such as the US, China, Sweden, Great Britain, Italy and India. It is argued that commercialization of organ donation is perceived as a real threat and danger by transplant legislation in most countries and therefore, trading of organs is penalized by almost all of them. Fluss informs that the conference on Health Policy, Ethics and Human Values convened at Noordwijk, Netherlands by the Council for International Organisation of Medical Sciences (CIOMS) in collaboration with WHO strongly recommended the banning of payments for any kind of human tissues or organs removed from any living or dead person. Besides, transplant legislation enacted in 39 countries as well as declaration by the Council of Europe and the World Medical Associations proposed to put an end to such disgraceful practices as trading of organs (1991; 309).

However, despite the enactment of national and international laws which forbid monetary transactions in organs, news of malpractices in the system of organ donation continue to filter in from various parts of the world. In most countries, the legislation on organ donation is still groping and struggling to get out of the moral conflict between 'altruism' and 'market' forces.

The conflict is far too controversial to get settled in the legal domain.

In examining the above ethical issues, the importance of the cultural dimension of organ transplantation has been emphasized. This is because our objective is to study organ transplantation from the sociological perspective to underline the fact that transplantation is a social process. It is a medical therapy that involves interchange between individuals – an extra ordinary interchange of organs. It has necessitated the need for individuals to recognize their dependence on each other. It has generated the need for sociological investigation into the socio-cultural environment within which this interchange of organs takes place.

"Cross cultural evidence reveals that human body parts of living as well as dead donors are often considered to be of great social worth" (Sharp 1995; 361). But since the same body parts are subject to different cultural interpretations in different cultures, there is a need to understand and investigate into the various cultural perspectives that regulate the giving and receiving of organs. The different cultural understandings of biological facts of life and death, as provided in this study, question the acceptance of these issues as 'natural facts of life'. Once an understanding of these crucial issues related to transplantation is achieved, it will become possible to know the cultural factors that hinder the acceptance of transplantation in particular cultures. Accordingly, steps could be taken to ensure that organ transplantation is undertaken in a manner consistent with the ethical beliefs and practices of the people in these cultures. Perhaps, it would lead to the establishment of ethical guidelines that would provide the medical therapy of transplantation to the people without violating their moral principles.

This study focuses on a few ethical and policy questions related to organ transplantation. It leaves out some of the medico-ethical issues such as : How and in what circumstances a volunteer donor could be considered free from social obligations? What are the ethical issues involved in procuring and administering life saving drugs to a transplant patient? How can the quality of life be improved after organ transplantation? How should the rights of prisoners, lunatics, old and handicapped be protected? What are the alternative therapies to transplantation? What are the coping strategies of families of patients advised kidney transplantation? How should promotional campaigns be organized to generate awareness about transplantation? How far is it ethical to destroy an animal in order to prolong a human life? How could medical technology be improved to provide better treatment to organ failure patients? What protection do medical men require from society and law in the improvement of transplant technology? Do they require ethical guidelines in extending the benefits of organ transplant to the people? To what extent must the state bear the economic cost of clinical organ transplantation? How much money should be allocated by the state to organ transplant procedures?

The present study addresses itself to the following:

* Given that the demand for transplantable organs far exceeds the supply, what are the ethical issues and perspectives responsible for the limited availability of organs in a society.
* How can the supply of organs be increased - by propagating the gift or the market ideology.
* Which policy on organ transplantation is likely to increase motivation to donate without violating moral principles.

Such issues cannot indeed be addressed without raising an ethical and moral debate between the principles of society and culture on one hand and the needs of medicine and technology on the other which we have done in this study. Keeping this into consideration, this study is presented with the hope that it will help in the understanding of a vital medical issue with important social ramifications created by medical technological advances.

2

ETHICAL ISSUES AND PERSPECTIVES

Organ transplantation, all over the world, is recognized as a successful medical surgery through which parts from one individual are used to replace dysfunctional ones in others (Sharp 1995; 357). According to Stickel, "The main principle upon which transplantation as a form of treatment is based is the principle of replacement. In situations wherein a disease is confined to one part of the body and that part of the body is damaged beyond repair, the restoration of health depends upon some form of replacement of that part" (1967; 37). Organ replacement therapy developed by the transplantation technique has given rise to the concept of what Joralemon calls "body as a collection of replaceable parts" (1995, 335). Hogle (in Williams 1997; 1043) noted that "body parts are becoming increasingly 'widget' like, that is, standardized items to be replaced as needed on demand... In this way, they are becoming not only substitutable mechanical parts but more like off-the-shelf reagents available for use in a variety of end users" (1995, 208). This, according to Knutson, has led to increased demands for human bodies and body parts for variety of purposes such as teaching, therapeutic demonstration and research as well as their preservation in body banks for transplantation (1968; 394). As Hogle argues, "it is through such medical practices of converting body parts into usable therapeutic tools that cultural meanings of human body emerge"(1996; 676).

There exists substantial cultural opposition to the use of body parts as therapeutic tools which has compelled the medical and anthropological community to recognize the link between transplant surgery and socio-cultural norms and values. In many societies and cultures several ethico-cultural questions have arisen about the use of body parts for transplantation. These questions relate to the beliefs concerning body integrity, personhood, cultural understandings of life and death. The importance of studying transplantation in its socio-cultural context has been recognized by a variety of scholars such as : Daar and Marshall (1998), Rothman (1998), Sharp (1995), Joralemon (1995), Ohnuki-Tierney (1994), Livingston (1993), Hogle (1996), Gabr (1998) and Feldman (1988). It is primarily the views of these scholars that will be discussed here.

Among the most compelling issues is the ethico-moral dilemma that surrounds organ transplantation. According to Sharp, the unravelling of this moral dilemma reveals cultural values societies assign to the body (1995; 357). Here, it is important to note that there is no uniform concept of the body across cultures. As Mary Douglas says (in Benoist and Cathebras), "The social body (that is, the societal and religious notion of the body) constrains the way the physical body (that is, the body perceived through its function) is perceived. The physical experience of the body, always modified by the social categories through which it is known, sustains a particular view of society" (Benoist and Cathebres 1993; 858). Douglas' statement draws our attention to the need to study the cultural construction of the social body and how the socio-cultural value of bodies and their parts constrain or facilitate the availability of organs for transplantation. In this chapter we examine the various cultural issues involved in both live as well as cadaveric organ transplantation. We discuss cross cultural perspectives on death and cadaveric organ donation and examine how the new physiological criterion of certifying death by the cessation of brain activity (brain death), evolved by the medical scientists to make organs available for transplantation meets resistance from the community. An attempt is also made to carry forward the Durkheimian tradition by following the arguments of Durkheim's student - Robert Hertz who differentiated simple from complex societies depending on their attitude towards death. However, in this chapter, a case is made for differentiating not only between simple and complex societies but also the various industrially advanced complex societies depending upon their differential conceptualizations of death.

We shall first take up live organ donation in the context of kidney transplantation which is, undoubtedly, the most unique advancement in the field of medicine because the surgery performed on the donor, involving considerable pain and inconvenience, is not for his own physical or medical benefit. Kidney transplantation is greatly influenced by the cultural beliefs about significance and function of kidneys which vary across cultures. In China, for example, Ikels argues that these concerns are augmented by widely held beliefs about the significance and function of the kidney derived from traditional medical concepts. According to Ikels, traditional medical beliefs are so powerful that almost no live donations occur in China (1997; 1274).

According to 'The Essential Book of Traditional Chinese Medicine Volume I Theory' which is used in China to teach medical students about traditional medicine:

> The Kidney stores genuine 'Yin' and 'Yang' or vital essence and vital function. Vital essence is the material basis of life. It is composed of two parts : reproductive essence, which controls reproduction and the essence of the 'Zang fu' organs, which controls growth, development and other life activities. The first of these is acquired from one's parents and the second is produced by the spleen and stomach. Both are stored in the kidney.

> Chinese medicine explains the kidney essence as kidney 'qi'. The rise and fall of kidney 'qi' influences reproduction, growth and development.
>
> Chinese medicine also speaks of a 'vital gate' which is viewed as the source of life. The 'fire' or source of energy of the vital gate is kidney. This is the dynamic source of reproduction and development as well as the source of energy for all the other organs (Ikels 1997; 1274).

According to the Chinese belief, "one could not transfer kidneys between the sexes without causing sexual confusion on the part of the recipient. A woman who received a man's kidney would, due to different harmones produced, find herself attracted to her own sex as would a man who received a woman's kidney" (Ikels 1997; 1275).

Apart from such ethico-medical issues, living organ donation is severely hampered by the legal criterion in counties such as India where receiving an organ (kidney) from a live donor other than one's near relative (including father, mother, sister, brother, son, daughter, spouse) is legally banned. This has, in turn, resulted in proliferation of illegal trading in kidneys. This aspect will be discussed in Chapter 4. Many countries such as the United States, Britain, Italy and Sweden rely on the policy of voluntary donation. So long as the kidney has been voluntarily given by a living donor, the donors or the recipients do not invite legal penalty although it is questionable and open to suspicion whether all donations of organs are, indeed, voluntarily made (that is, not governed by any obligation to give or receive an organ). Moreover, it is unlikely that monetary considerations are not involved between live donor and recipient in these nations. Due to lack of empirical studies and literature on this aspect, such an issue has not been discussed here.

Since most of the transplantable organs except kidneys and some part of the liver cannot be donated by living beings, procurement of most organs is dependent on donations from cadavers. "With patient demand for transplantation so strong and the medical capacity to satisfy it so widespread", Rothman argues that "most of the doctors and others involved in early transplants expected that organs would be readily donated from the dead - a giving that cost the donor nothing - and brought the recipient obvious advantages. However, it turns out that powerful cultural and religious taboos discourage cadaveric organ donations not only in countries with strong religious establishments but even in more secular ones as well" (Rothman 1998; 14).

The major controversy surrounding the issue of cadaveric organ donation is related to the new medical criterion of certifying clinical death by the cessation of brain function of an individual (that is, brain death) which makes it possible to remove 'living' organs from the clinically dead person. According to Keithmant, increasing practice of organ transplantation together with the developments in artificial means for maintaining breathing and circulation have introduced a new dimension to diagnosis of death whereby a person is declared dead by the cessation of his brain functions (1965; 29). Similarly, Waltz and Ibau argue that traditionally, death was said to have taken place, medically, whenever it could be declared that both the heart and lungs had irrevocably ceased to function. This phenomenon is generally referred to as 'clinical death'. Today primarily because of advances in transplantation, it has been suggested that death be redefined as 'brain death' (1971; 228). Defining the term 'brain death', Bavinck says, "it is used to refer to the definitive and irreparable cessation of brain function. This is the case when there is no longer any spontaneous respiration and the patient is dependent on a respirator. The body is no longer able to maintain blood pressure and temperature and does not respond to administered pain stimuli. These are the strict criteria for establishing 'brain death' and this is done by independent physicians who are not involved in the transplantation" (1996; 76).

According to Bavinck, the moment at which 'brain death' is established and declared by the physician is considered the official time of death and it is very significant in the context of transplantation (1996; 77). By defining death as 'brain death', medical scientists argue that it would be possible to procure organs from individuals whose brains are dead but other organs such as heart, liver, lung, kidneys, eyes, pancreas etc. are living and are medically suitable to be transplanted into the body of a person suffering from organ failure (Bavinck 1996; 77). According to Waltz and Ibau, the time lapse between donor death and organ use is of crucial significance in the context of organ transplantation (1971; 228). As per the medical criterion, kidneys, heart, liver and lungs to be transplanted must be removed within 30 minutes of the donor's death (Waltz and Ibau 1971; 228). If a patient who has been declared 'brain dead' had indicated prior to his death that he wished his organs to be made available for transplantation, then, he is placed on a respirator and the vital organs are kept alive by artificial means (Bavinck 1996; 77).

Ohnuki-Tierney states that anthropologists have always emphasized that death is not an objective or culture free state. The question of when life ends and death begins is enormously complex (1994; 235). This can be supported by various citations by Poe, Medawar and Newsweek, as quoted in Giacomini. According to Allen Poe "the boundaries which divide life from death are, at best, shadowy and vague. Who shall say where the one ends and where the other begins". Similarly, Brian Medawar states, "Legally, I suppose a man is dead when he has undergone irreversible changes of a type that make it impossible for him to seek to litigate". However, Newsweek (1967, 18 Dec., 87) reports, "You're dead when your doctor says you are" (Giacomini 1997; 1465).

Angrosino argues that there does not exist a single, clearly defined and universal method for defining and diagnosing death.

She shows that death is also a result of negotiation among various interested parties in context specific interactions - that is, the recipient of an organ and his/her family and transplant surgeons in need of organs. The surgeons may define it in one way whereas relatives of a dying patient who may be unwilling to pay for prolonged and intensive care of a dead brain in the live body may look for another definition (1994; 243). According to her, "the decision to declare death is evidently a social act that occurs in various ways depending upon shifting circumstances. It is not purely an exercise of neutral biomedical technology" (Angrosino 1994; 243).

Ohnuki-Tierney argues that the biological death and social death are two different life events which may or may not coincide. The physiological death of a person (that is, the loss of physical functions such as the stoppage of brain or respiratory activities) may not necessarily constitute his social death (that is, from the social point of view) (1994; 235). This ambiguity is also found in the new medical criterion of declaring a person 'brain dead'. As Ohnuki-Tierney argues, 'brain death' is a new phenomenon determined by social agents in each culture (1994; 234). There are several societies that do not accept 'brain death' as determining the death of a person. For example, in Israel, according to Rothman, "orthodox Jewish precepts define death exclusively as the failure of the heart to function, not the cessation of brain activity, a standard that makes it almost impossible to retrieve organs. Some Rabbis do give precedence to saving a life and would therefore accept the standard of 'brain death' for transplantation but overall rates of donation in Israel are very low" (1998; 14).

According to Inwald, Jakobivits and Petros, the Jews beleive that the breathing function is crucial for defining the moment of death. For example, the physical decapitation of an animal determines death even if there is some degree of subsequent movement like the severed tail of a lizard that twitches spasmodically. Similarly, in the case of an individual trapped under a fallen building, the absence of breathing may determine death even if cessation of the heartbeat is not established. According to them, the progressive Jews (who accept brain stem death as a valid determinant of death within the Jewish tradition) argue that it is physiologically equivalent to decapitation - that destruction of the brain stem means inability to breathe spontaneously. As against this view, the majority of Jews still believe that brain stem death is not the equivalent of anatomical decapitation and that the coordinated beating of the heart and maintenance of blood circulation in a brain dead person is no different from the beating of the heart in a normal individual. According to them, death occurs only when there is neither breathing nor cardiac pulsation. Since this is not the case in a brain stem dead patient on a ventilator, these patients cannot be considered dead. (Inwald et al.; 2000-1267). This is the majority view according to Inwald et al.; in the orthodox Jewish tradition and it is summed up by the former Chief Rabbi of the United Kingdom and expert on Jewish medical ethics, Lord Jakobovits (in Inwald et al.) as follows :

> "So long as the heart still functions and the blood circulates, death has not yet set in. But this does not mean that a lingering life, especially when experiencing great pain, must be prolonged at all costs and in all circumstances... On the responsibility for making such decisions... affecting life and death, it should be emphasized that these should, wherever possible, be left to disinterested parties, preferably including experts, including moral specialists such as experienced Rabbinic authorities" (Inwald et al. 2000; 1267).

Japan, according to Ohnuki-Tierney, has not yet passed legislation equating 'brain death' with the death of a person. As a result cadaveric transplants are performed very infrequently in comparison with the situation in the United States, the United Kingdom and France. The Japanese, according to her, do not recognize 'brain death' partly because they are skeptical whether such a death can be determined with certainty. Although they consider each condition medically used to define 'brain death' as necessary criterion yet they insist that the sum of these conditions is not enough to declare a person dead. For the Japanese and for many other people, before the notion of 'brain death' emerged, the inactive brain represented a prolongation of life rather than a prolongation of the process of dying as it has come to be viewed in some western countries (1994; 234). Japanese resistance, according to Ohnuki-Tierney, derives to a large degree from the fact that the concept of 'brain death' brought about by the new medical technology represents a concept of death that is deeply embedded in a western intellectual tradition that is quite alien because for them, "the body is more than an appendage of the brain" (1994; 234).

Feldman (1988) informs that the ancient belief systems of Japan– Shinto and Buddhism offer resistance to the acceptance of 'brain death' as constituting the death of a person. Describing the idea of the freshly dead prevalent in Shinto belief, Feldman states, "there is a period of 49 days during which the soul of the deceased is thought to be polluted by death and was neither part of the living nor of the ancestors" (1988; 341). In contrast to this, he says, "Brain death makes radically different assumptions about the specificity of the dying process. It pinpoints a number of critical medical factors and draws a sharp distinction between life and death" (Feldman 1988; 341).

Indicating a central tenet of 'ancestor worship' prevalent in the Shinto belief system, Feldman states, "the welfare of the living is dependent upon paying appropriate homage to the dead. So long as the deceased is given the proper offerings and honored by suitable funeral arrangements, then the living suffer no ill. But declaring a person dead based on a brain dead criterion may not be the most respectful way in which to treat one's future ancestors and cutting up their bodies in order to harvest their organs clearly violates the respect that is their due" (1988; 342). Therefore, he argues that the notion of 'brain death' and harvesting organs from the bodies of the dead encounters strong resistance and rejection from the Japanese (Feldman 1988; 341).

Rothman states, "For all its interest in new technology and its traditions of gift giving, Japan has only a minuscule program, devoted almost exclusively to transplanting kidneys from living related donors" (1998; 14). In the context of cadaveric organ donation in Japan, Lock (in Rothman 1998; 14) argues that the idea of having a deceased relative whose body is not complete prior to burial or cremation is associated with misfortune because in this situation suffering in the other world never terminates.

The Japanese, according to Ohnuki-Tierney, are particularly concerned about the intactness of the body expressed as 'gotai' - the five body parts. The notion is closely related to the Japanese taboo on violence to the body which causes imbalance. This is evident from a variety of cultural practices prevalent in Japan, e.g., when the Japanese adopted technology, city planning, the legal system and many other socio-cultural institutions from China during the fifth and sixth centuries, they did not adopt ear piercing or foot binding. Even today, ear piercing is uncommon, although some young woman and a smaller number of young men have lately adopted this fashion. Those whose 'gotai' is missing or deformed termed as 'gotai fugu', have encountered considerable cultural and social discrimination especially in the past (1994; 235).

According to Ohnuki-Tierney, the Japanese are particularly concerned with the intactness of the body after death. This notion saw formal expression in the Confucian doctrine that the intact 'gotai' guaranteed the rebirth of the soul. The Japanese eagerness to cremate the dead bodies as early as possible is partly attributable to the importance of 'gotai'. It facilitates a swift transformation of 'gotai'. The warriors' practice of taking the enemy's head also derives from this notion. Beheading constituted the ultimate killing because by violating the integrity of the body, it prevented the enemy's rebirth. For many Japanese, the removal of organs from dead bodies violates the integrity of the body of the deceased. The 'gotai' notion also underlies the Japanese reluctance to consider implants. To date, no implanted pace maker has been manufactured in Japan. In the view of Japanese, implants remain alien to the body which disturbs the integrity of the body (1994; 236).

Although Americans tend to favor transplantation, they seem to be quite reluctant to donate organs. This is evident from the low organ donation rates witnessed in America. According to Christiansen et. al, "nearly 53,000 Americans are awaiting organ transplants. Only 20,109 transplants were performed in 1994. The waiting list for organs grew at an annual rate of 15.5% between 1988 and 1994, while the number of transplants performed grew 6.7% per year. The death toll among transplant candidates exceeded 3,500 in 1995 and has been growing at an annual rate of 13.0%. The national donor potential, on the other hand, is estimated between 6,900 and 10,700 cases per year (1998; 1645).

The problem is especially severe in the context of black Americans as reported in various studies. For example, Livingston reported a low rate of donation among black and hispanic populations. He found that patients who were treated at institutions that served a predominantly white population were almost twice as likely to receive a transplantable organ as patients who were treated at institutions that served a predominantly black population. According to him, the two major reasons why a potential black donor does not become an actual donor, are lack of referral and lack of consent (1993; 617). Callender (in Livingston 1993; 617) reported the attitudes of 40 black men and women towards organ donation and identified five reasons for the low donation rate among blacks - lack of awareness about organ and tissue donation, religious fears, myths and superstitions, distrust of the medical community, fear of premature death and racism (blacks wanted to receive and donate organs to other blacks) (1993; 617). Creecy and Wright also report that black Americans rarely volunteer as organ donors (1990; 1231).

Based on the information received from black organ procurement specialists, Prottas (in Livingston 1993; 618) reported that the blacks have specific race related fears about organ donation. For example, they fear that after agreeing to donate their organs, they will be exposed to undesirable behaviour by the hospital personnel who will hasten their death. They also believe that organ donation only helps the whites who are the prime recipients of the donated organs and not the blacks. The relatively low organ donation rates among blacks, thus, counter and negate the popular view that Americans have a positive attitude towards organ donation (Livingston 1993; 618).

The literary critic Leslie-Fiedler (in Rothman, 1998; 15) suggests that the unwillingness of Americans to donate organs reflects an underlying antipathy to science and a fear of artificially creating life - a fear exploited in many Hollywood stories and also that donation would force Americans to concede the finality of death which they are reluctant to do. Commenting on Fiedler's suggestions, Rothman argues that the underlying causes are less psychological than social. Americans are actually unaccustomed to sharing resources of any kind when it comes to medicine. Since Americans refuse to care for one another in life, why would they do so in death? As he argues, "receiving help is one thing, donating it is another" (1998; 15).

Knutson (1968; 397) argues that Americans' attitude towards autopsies and uses of the dead body or body parts are rooted in their beliefs about the sanctity of the body, beliefs about the existence and nature of a human soul and beliefs about the definition of a human life. With respect to beliefs pertaining to the sanctity of the body, the informants in his study took the following position based on the reading of the old testament -

> ...God created man in his image.
>
> The image of God - Man - should not be cut open and examined after death but should remain sacred.
>
> For dust thou art and unto dust shalt thou return
> Then shall the dust return to the earth as it was : and the spirit shall return unto God who gave it (Knutson 1968; 397-398).

Hogle, on the other hand, argues that Americans are a little less antithetical to the idea of obtaining organs from dead bodies than other cultures because in the United States there is high cultural value placed on technological progress which has brought bodily materials into the realm of commodities. This is evident from the fact that a number of explicit market mechanisms are currently being proposed for the exchange of body organs and tissues. Also, a variety of American practices and techniques are currently being developed specifically for making use of materials from dead bodies. Therefore, under such conditions where technological progress is considered a virtue, as in the United States, medical authority of transplantation and the use of cadaveric body materials is relatively unchallenged (1996; 676). Ohnuki-Tierney also opines that in the United States transplants of cadaveric organs have been so naturalized that they are no longer newsworthy (1994; 233).

In the context of Germany, Hogle argues that particular historical, social and political contexts have made the procurement of human materials from brain dead bodies a highly contested practice. He reports that Germany is witnessing an ideological cultural debate regarding the use of body materials. On the one hand are those people who argue for maintaining racial hygiene by not donating their body organs to new immigrants and on the other are those who argue for maintaining altruism in the society by giving one's organs to others for social good and, thus, helping the new immigrants. These circumstances have led the Germans to ask, "After all what exactly is the social good? And to whom do we owe what?" (1996; 678).

The drive to use human organs and tissues as effective therapeutic tools is further constrained in Germany by the need to maintain cultural values of bodily integrity and personhood dignity, both during life time and after death, which is essentially linked to their cultural conception of human body as divine creation. In a study conducted by Hogle on the use of human body organs after death, German respondents said that, in order to be functional, human materials needed to be 'lebensfrish' - that is, fresh from the body and, thus, closer to the live and natural state (1996;678). Germans, thus, conceive of human bodily materials as natural products that have been naturally produced by God and are therefore strictly against such medical procedures that appear to violate bodily integrity and dignity (Hogle 1996;680). Since both the processes of giving as well as receiving of organs for transplantation require an intrusion into the bodies of both living and dead patients, they are considered to be extreme violations of bodily dignity which has attracted widespread resentment in Germany as it is clear from Hogle's study where families of intensive care patients were increasingly hostile towards physicians saying such things as "we will watch you - you will get no organs from my family member" (1996; 678).

Deutsches (in Hogle 1996; 677) states that Germans are particularly against cadaveric organs procurement because of several sensational stories that have developed around the use of dead human bodies. One such story, according to Deutsches, revealed that cadaveric parts such as bone and other tissues are being routinely sold to pharmaceutical firms by pathology assistants and that they are profitably marketed by them (Hogle 1996; 677).

In China, Ikels argues that Buddhism could reasonably be expected to be sympathetic rather than antagonistic to the generous act of donation to enhance the prospects of a favouable rebirth by the donor. Yet, in reality, he says, few people seem to be motivated to donation on either of these grounds (1997; 1276). However, Rahul Gupta - a journalist, reports in 'The Times of India', "Buddhists believe that the body does not belong to the person and hence donate organs willingly" (August 13, 2000). Further, Ikels says that in China, Confucianism is frequently cited as a major reason for Chinese reluctance to donate. Specifically, the central concept of filial piety is said to require individuals to return the body to the ancestors in the same intact state in which they received it from their parents. Thus, donating either one's own or a family member's corpse is likely to meet with strong objections from others. Wanting to return the body intact to the ancestors is usually the first reason people offer for Chinese reluctance to donate cadavers. Logically, it could also be a factor inhibiting live donation (1997; 1276).

According to Ikels, people working in the field of dissection, who are necessarily on the front lines when it comes to acquiring corpses are more likely to mention 'feudal superstitions' such as beliefs about ghosts as a major barrier to donation and to call for efforts to eradicate such erroneous and deleterious beliefs. Three beliefs, he says, are particularly important in this context. First is the belief that the corpse might need all its body parts to traverse the underworld successfully enroute to its final reward. As an example of this type of worry, an informant in a study conducted by Ikels in Taiwan related a dream in which a deceased grandfather had complained that because his glasses had not been burned as part of the funeral ritual and thereby sent to him in the spirit world, he had difficulty finding his way around. Second is the belief that a ghost subjected to autopsy or deprived of its organs might become angry and retaliate against those who authorized the use of its body in this way. Third is the belief that the ghost does not rest, until the corpse is buried or if cremated, placed in a container for ashes. If it does not happen, it remains among the living until that time, quite possibly in an agitated state and fully aware of what is going on (1997; 1276).

In the context of organ donation in China, another issue that is important, according to Ikels, is the nature of death. According to him, "the traditional folk religion allows that some people by the very nature of their deaths, will become angry ghosts. These are largely people who have died before their time through accidents, homicides, suicides or executions. The ghosts of those who die by suicide are especially feared as they are believed to have left this world already angry and itching to get even with whosoever drove them to take their lives. Coincidentally, in the eyes of the medical profession these types of deaths are precisely the ones most likely to produce a suitable organ donor as the deceased is probably young, vigorous and otherwise healthy until his or her sudden demise. Furthermore, in the case of dissection, the body can be kept at a morgue for a substantial length of time whereas in the case of transplantation, the body must be utilized almost immediately" (1997, 1276).

Further, Ikels informs that it is not easy to discern whether refusal to give consent for organ donation is a matter of filial piety in China or of fear of ghosts but it is clear that Chinese are strictly against altering the bodies of their dead (1997;1276-1277). As he states, "one Hong Kong physician related that obtaining consent for autopsy can be very difficult - that in one case, a family member knelt down before him pleading that he not perform the autopsy. Much more well known is the Chinese aversion to cremation. The Chinese government has successfully imposed this form of body disposition in China but people employ every conceivable strategy to avert this fate for their relatives" (Ikels 1997; 1277).

In the middle east, according to Rothman, it is rare to obtain organs from cadavers because Islamic teachings emphasize the need to maintain the integrity of the body after death and although some prominent religious leaders make an exception for transplant by stressing the altruistic aspect of organ donations by calling it 'the gift of life', most others refuse it. As Rothman mentions, "an intense debate occurred in March 1997 in Egypt when the government appointed leader of the most important Sunni Muslim theological faculty endorsed transplantation as an act of altruism saying that permitting it was to accept a small harm in order to avoid a greater harm - the same rationale that allows a Muslim to eat pork if he risks starvation but other cleriks immediately objected to it and there is no agreement in favour of donation till date" (1998; 14).

Further, in Islamic countries, according to Daar (in Ohnuki-Tierney 1994; 238), the rights of the community take precedence over the rights of the individual. Islamic law dictates that the body of the deceased be buried on the day of death. Individuals in these countries are, therefore, not free agents making independent decisions about the disposal of their bodies. If a person's organ is transplanted to another individual, it must, nevertheless, be buried according to Islamic law when the recipient dies. This poses problems if the recipient belongs to another religion in which case the transplanted organ must be removed so that it can be buried on the day of the recipient's death. Thus, according to Islamic culture, donors may offer their organs but the organs donated remain under the jurisdiction of their communities and, thus, under Islamic law (Ohnuki-Tierney 1994; 238).

In India, Vibha Sharma - a journalist, stated in 'Hindustan Times' that the mythological and religious beliefs hinder the donation of cadaveric organs for transplantation as people fear that the departed soul would not achieve *moksha* (salvation) if his organs are not purified with the rest of his body in the holy flames of the funeral pyre (December 10, 2000). Similarly, Rahul Gupta - a journalist, reported in 'The Times of India' that one reason eye donations are not popular in India is because of the superstitions and social norms. According to him, people believe that removal of their eyes would mean that they will be born blind in the next life (August 13, 2000). The above observations, thus, support Ikels' statement that "there is currently a major disjunction between the thinking of those in the medical profession (or atleast of those in the most technologically advanced areas) and the bulk of the population. While the doctors are more concerned with ending patient's suffering, the laymen are more constrained by cultural fears such as bodily impurity, ghosts of the dead, intactness of the body etc. Thus, the medical scientists are caught in a dilemma" (1997; 1277). Waltz and Ibau argue that "It ...would be medically, legally and ethically wrong to do anything at the expense of the life or the comfort of the dying patient who is a prospective donor just to secure a healthy transplant" (1971; 228). According to them, a medical man is also required not to delay the pronouncement of death for insubstantial cultural reasons where such a delay may jeopardize treatment of a transplant recipient (Waltz and Ibau1971; 228).

Given the cultural constraints on cadaveric organ donation described above, several solutions and strategies to increase organ donation have been proposed by transplant professionals, medical ethicists and a variety of other scholars. Some of these strategies, as suggested by Ikels, include discouraging traditional beliefs and customs, promoting the acceptance of the concept of 'brain death', promoting knowledge of the importance of dissection, providing incentives to cadres, medical workers and potential donors and demonstrating the benefits of organ transplantation by bringing organ recipients into the public arena (1997; 1280).

It may be suggested that promotional campaigns, meetings and discussions should be organized such as those organized by national and international transplant games federations where general public is informed about the benefits of transplantation and encouraged to donate organs. According to Fracs and Richard, a cross curriculum programme for secondary schools has been developed in Australia with an education package involving comprehensive teaching notes and a video containing case studies. The students are encouraged to discuss these issues in the family environment (1990; 139). It is expected that this program will profoundly influence community attitude and awareness about organ donation and transplantation in the years to come. It should, however, be remembered that the religious, cultural and ethnic attitudes of people towards death developed over centuries and to change those attitudes to achieve any kind of consensus between the medical and cultural values will no doubt take several years.

Veatch argues that terms such as 'brain death' and 'heart death' are in themselves quite ambiguous. These can mean the death of the individual based on the irreversible destruction of the brain or heart but these can also mean the death of a part of organ (such as the heart or a brain) in a still living person. Since the living person with a dead heart or brain may be treated quite differently - legally, ethically, socially, culturally and psychologically from a dead person, the terms 'brain death' and 'heart death' should not be used. To refer to the death of a person (as a whole), he suggests that one should refer to the death of that person based on brain or heart criterion (1989; 17).

To define the death of a human being, Veatch argues that we must recognize its essential human characteristics - the loss of which determines his death. To ask what is essentially significant to a human being is a philosophical question - a question of ethical and cultural values. Therefore, any concept of death will depend upon how a particular socio-cultural system evaluates essential human characteristics (1989; 16-17).

In societies such as Israel, China or Japan, taking organs from a person who has been declared brain dead by medical professionals would be equivalent to killing or murdering him because the person is not yet considered socially dead. He may in the eyes of his family and society, still be living, e.g. for the Japanese, according to Ohnuki-Tierney, the cessation of brain activity does not mean prolongation of the process of dying but the prolongation of the process of living so that taking organs from a brain stem dead person would be equal to killing him (1994; 234-235).

Similarly, in China, Ikels informs that people refuse to accept 'brain death' as constituting the death of a person because the brain dead patient is maintained on a respirator, he looks very much alive and is still warm, its chest goes up and down and there is a pulse and urine is produced (1997; 1277).

Ohnuki-Tierney argues that the death of a member of the social group is a significant occasion on which cherished values, emotions and human relationships are called forth (1994; 235). According to Hertz (in Taylor and Ashworth 1987; 42), those societies where death initiates a prolonged institutionalized series of rituals, often involving considerable financial and human costs, may be called simple societies characterized by mechanical solidarity in Durkheimian terms. These may be contrasted with complex industrialized societies characterized by organic solidarity, that is, by the absence of such elaborate mortuary rituals (Taylor and Ashworth 1987; 42) .

We shall next examine the extent to which the dominant theoretical perspective in medical sociology - namely society's attitude towards death, represents an advance on Durkheim's ideas. To illustrate the Durkheimian approach, the work of his pupil Robert Hertz (as it appeared in Taylor and Ashworth 1987; 42) may be cited. Hertz (in Taylor and Ashworth 1987; 42) observed that "...death does not confine itself to the ending of bodily life, it is thus a social event; its nature and consequences depend on how it is represented in the belief systems of society" (1987; 42).

"In modern society", according to Hertz, "we tend to conceive death as the opposite to life. We treat it as an essentially individual inter personal event brought about by natural causes and marked by a single ritual ceremony of mourning which signifies permanent withdrawal from 'this world'. These representations of death are not universal but particular... In the primitive societies... examined by Hertz, death (other than by wounds) is not seen as a natural phenomenon but as caused by spiritual powers, either because the deceased had violated a taboo or been the victim of an enemy sorcerer in which case the death becomes part of a sinister plot" (Taylor and Ashworth 1987; 42).

"Further, in contrast to the modern complex societies, in societies characterized by mechanical solidarity, the group loses a part of itself by death (Taylor and Ashworth 1987;42)". As Hertz puts it : "It seems that the entire community feels itself lost or atleast directly threatened by the presence of antagonistic forces and the very basis of its existence is shaken" (Taylor and Ashworth 1987; 42).

As Taylor and Ashworth argue, "Hertz's analysis is typically Durkheimian; the linking of different kinds of individual experiences and social actions to the collective consciousness, the stress on function..., the use of comparative method and the focus on an aspect of social reality to make general observations about the nature of the whole... his brilliant essay on death is enought to indicate the extent to which the study of attitudes to death, mourning and ritualistic mortuary practices can reveal important aspects of the nature of social solidarity and its changing forms. Thus, just as Durkheim used the study of law as an index of the change from mechanical to organic solidarity (1933), so a Durkheimien inspired medical sociologist could usefully undertake a historical and cross cultural study using responses to death as an indicator of different forms of the collective conscience" (1987; 42).

In furthering Durkheimian tradition, analysis of death may be carried forward to argue that a society's attitude to death can be used to differentiate not just simple and complex societies but also various complex modern societies. This is so because some industrially advanced societies which possess both the financial and the technical capacity to adopt transplant technology are resistant to the new medical criterion of 'brain death' while there are others for whom 'brain death' is nothing but a naturalized medical procedure developed to save thousands of ill fated diseased human lives. Thus, we note that societies such as Japan, Israel and China that are industrially advanced are still opposed to this notion of 'brain death'. On the other hand, there are industrially advanced societies such as US and UK that accept 'brain death' as constituting the death of an individual. Thus, the cultural altitudes and responses of different advanced societies vary widely. Ohnuki-Tierney also states that America seems to accept 'brain death' as a medically definable condition that can be diagnosed with certainty to constitute the death of the person. The Japanese, by contrast, refuse the recognize 'brain death' as biological death of a person because they remain skeptical whether 'brain death' can be determined with certainty. According to her, there are societies such as the United States, the United Kingdom and France which provide a sympathetic environment for medical professionals to pursue transplantation of human organs due to their recognition and acceptance of 'brain death'. On the other hand, there are societies such as Israel, Denmark and Japan that remain resistant to the new medical technology of transplantation due to their resistance to the concept of brain death (1994; 233-234).

In Ohnuki-Tierney's view, the notion of death, although framed as highly scientific and culture free, is actually culturally constructed (1994; 234). It is in this sense that differential cultural perspectives on death can be used as important indicators of different forms of collective conscience, in the Durkheimian sense. It can be used to differentiate not just simple and complex societies but also different types of complex societies.

The point being stressed in this chapter is that an understanding of cultural perspectives on organ procurement and transplantation is important if transplant therapy is to receive a favourable cultural response from the society in which it is introduced to treat organ failure patients. In this chapter, we discussed cross cultural perspectives on death and cadaveric organ donation and showed how the societal norms, values, ethics and beliefs attached to such issues as life and death, bodies, and body parts can provide strong opposition to the acceptance and development of transplantation as a successful medical procedure.

The cultural resistance encountered by the new medical criterion of death based on the cessation of brain function has necessitated the need to evolve consensus between the cultural concept of death and the medical criterion of 'brain death'. One such consensual solution, as proposed by a lawyer in Japan, is mentioned by Feldman. According to the lawyer, an 'alpha period' should be recognized between the declaration of 'brain death' and the stoppage of the heart as a compromise between 'brain death' and more traditional views of death. This period, he says, is "supposed to lie between life and death belonging to neither and is meant to suggest that complete death may not immediately follow the death of the brain, that the body may for a while show features of both life and death" (Feldman 1988; 341).

The merits of such and other consensual solutions between cultural and medical notions of death cannot indeed be questioned. However, it remains to be seen whether such solutions will be actually successful in increasing the availability of organs for transplantation.

3
THE GIFT VERSUS THE MARKET IDEOLOGY

The supply of organs for transplantation has not kept pace with the increasing demand of organs for transplantation due to the improvement in medical technology. According to Horton and Horton, approximately, about one third of patients accepted for transplantation die, while waiting for a matching donor (1990; 791). The World Transplant Games Federation reports that in 1998, in the U.S. alone, there were 57,000 people waiting for an organ transplant, of whom 12% were children. In England, with a population of 55 million that comparison number was 5,100. In Italy, with a population of 57 million, there were 3,819 patients on the waiting list of whom 2,500 were waiting for a kidney. In Germany, France and Spain, the comparative figures were 39,000, 21,000 and 15,000 respectively. In Japan, 1,70,000 people were on dialysis, many of whom could be helped by a transplant. In India, according to Vij and Kalghatgi (1998), approximately 1,00,000 cases of kidney failure patients are identified every year but only about 1,500 donor kidneys are made available to them.

In this era of acute organ shortage, the transplant professionals are continuously searching for ways and means to increase the supply of transplantable organs[1]. Joralemon argues

1. Transplantable organs include heart, kidney, liver, lung and pancreas.

that the controversy over organ[2] procurement strategies reveals two extremely different and opposed sets of values invoked by the advocates of transplantation : altruism and individual rights (1995; 335). According to him, "at one extreme are those who view organ giving as gift giving and who search for ways to encourage altruism" (Joralemon 1995; 336). They are the advocates of the 'gift' ideology. For example, Livingston argues, "Altruism should be used as an appeal to direct and motivate organ donations among blacks in America" (1993; 364). In the context of blood donation, Titmuss argues, "...in complex, large scale societies... the application of scientific and technological developments... has increased... the social need for gift relationships... In many countries... there are countless numbers of voluntary ...donors ...there is no reason to doubt that many would respond by expressing... sentiments of altruism and reciprocity" (1970; 224). At the other extreme, Joralemon states are those who argue that human organs should be bought and sold like any other commodity in the market (1995; 336). They are the advocates of the 'market'or 'property rights' ideology (1995; 335). For example, while Rothman argues, "Why ban the sale of kidneys when the sale of other body parts such as hair, semen, female eggs and blood is allowed in many countries?" (1998; 15). Joraleman asks, "why shouldn't be individuals given full property rights over their bodies?" (1995; 340). Both the cultural metaphors, namely, 'gift giving' and 'property rights' according to Joralemon have been invoked as ideological supports for organ donation[3]. The idea, he believes, is, "to make use of the culturally familiar concepts and terminology so as to culturally legitimize clinical organ transplantation and, thus, make it seem to be fully consistent with the cultural meanings" (1995; 342).

---

2. In this chapter organ particularly refers to kidneys although some references are also made to heart and lungs.
3. Here, organ donation refers to both live as well as cadaveric donations of organs.

Joralemon further argues that the two ideologies although being in opposition to one another, begin from a common cultural baseline, that is, both recognize transplantation as an 'unquestioned good' and a 'triumph of medical science' which has challenged death (1995; 342). Hence, both share with each other their common concern for the shortage of organs which they argue can indeed be made up by encouraging people to give their organs either as gifts (as propagated by the 'gift' ideology) or in return for some financial or monetary compensation (as propagated by the 'market' ideology). Medically, both the solutions are feasible because there are sufficient number of persons dying every year in ways that would permit their organs to be reused for transplantation. According to Vij and Kalghatgi, there are many victims of traffic accidents whose heart has stopped beating or the brain has suffered irreversible damage who can provide sufficient number of kidneys for transplantation. In India alone, they argue, approximately 60,000 fatal accidents take place every year so even if the next of kin in 10% of these cases agree to donate organs around 12,000 kidneys would become available for transplantation (1998).

The Gift Ideology

The conception of organs as 'gifts' is found worldwide in the ways organ donation for transplantation is represented to the people by those transplant professionals, scholars and legal experts who seek to evoke the feelings and emotions of altruism among the donors of organs in order to encourage them to save a life rather than expect some reward or compensation.

According to Joralemon, "the gift ideology, is given its most dramatic presentation during the Transplant Games" (1995; 343). The transplant games are organized every second year to provide information and support to transplant patients in addition to educating them and enabling them to share their experiences and enjoying social activities, sports, etc. According to Joralemon, the 1994 transplant games in Atlanta, Georgia attracted around 1,050 participants of all ages and ethnicities from USA where the donors, the recipients, and all other participants wore T-shirts with messages such as 'recycle yourself' and 'sign up for life' (i.e. sign donor cards). Speaker after speaker at the opening ceremony referred to the 'second chance at life' made possible by the generosity of donors. They encouraged the public to 'share your life and share your decision'. The representatives of donor families were given flowers in gratitude and a 24 year old heart transplant recipient sang his own sentimental composition entitled 'The Gift of Life' (1995; 343). The transplant games held in Tilberg, the Netherlands in 1999 referred to transplant games as 'New Life Games'. Similarly the Ist SAARC Transplant Sports Meet and 5th All India Transplant Sports Meet held at Amritsar, India in 1998 used the logo 'back to life'. Moreover, the advertisement given by the World Transplant Games Federation to encourage organ donation is, 'Organ Gift, Life Gift'. Demonstrating the benefit of donating organs, the World Transplant Games Federation says via T.V., radio and news papers, "Look, these people are now well, should you deny them that chance? Do promise them the gift of life" (1998). Evidently, the ideology that is promoted in transplant games is undoubtedly the 'gift' ideology.

The intention behind propagating 'gift' ideology in organ donation is to encourage people to donate organs and serve humanity, that is, to think in terms of social good rather than personal benefit. The purpose is to distinguish the act of organ giving from commercial transaction. As Doctor Prem Aggarwal[4] puts it, "A kidney is not something that can be stolen, put into a refrigerator and used according to the doctor's convenience" (Vij and Kalghatgi 1998). Similarly Fluss argues, "donated organs should be made

4. Doctor Prem Aggarwal was the President of the Indian Medical Association at the time (Vij and Kalghatgi, 1998)

available to patients on the basis of medical need and not on the basis of financial or other consideration" (1991; 310). According to Joralemon, "the proponents of the gift ideology seek to connect organ donation to the sort of altruistic acts people perform during disasters and accidents. During such times, people extend caring responses without any expectation of repayment to the people affected by personal tragedies even though the individuals suffering are strangers. In other words, the gift ideologists associate organ donation to such cultural ideals as the generosity of strangers, the heroism of the person who risks life and limb to rescue those he or she does not know and the coming together of neighbourhoods in mutual support at moments of natural destruction" (1995; 344).

It is through these ideals, Sharp argues, that the 'gift' metaphor in the context of organ transplantation is expected to evoke such emotions as generosity, altruism and selflessness among the donors of organs (1995; 370). Altruistic behaviour according to Lightman, may be defined as action "carried out to benefit another without anticipation of rewards from external sources" (1982; 1628). The notion of altruism, however, comes out most significantly in the commonly used phrase for addressing organ donation, namely, 'giving the gift of life'. According to Sharp, the logic that inspires donating an organ as a gift is the fact that donor's kin can begin the bereavement process more quickly if they know that they have helped some one else. This is because the recipient gets a chance to live a longer, healthier and therefore, a more productive life because of the donated organ while the dead donor gets a chance to live another life through his donated organ in the recipient's body (1995; 364).

The 'gift' ideology is promoted by several people including transplant professionals, doctors, scholars, laymen, even donors and recipients themselves. E.g., in a National Organ and Tissue Donor Awareness Week held in U.S., 1999, an organ recipient stated, "Because of my gift from a 30 year old housewife who died of a bleeding aneurysm, I have celebrated 32 years of marriage, walked 3 daughters down the aisle in marriage and enjoyed 3 beautiful grandchildren. Shouldn't everyone on transplant lists enjoy the blessings that I received?" (Berry 1999; 1445). Similarly, Livingston argues, "Altruism should be used as an appeal to direct and motivate organ donations among blacks in America" (1993; 364).

According to Ohnuki-Tierney, the idea of donated organ as 'the gift of life' provides a moral framework within which the practice of organ donation is introduced to the people. These moral values, however, get their ultimate expression when religion sanctions organ donation as giving a gift of life (1994; 241). Horton and Horton quote from an article in 'The Christian Century' (1986) titled 'Theological vision statement from the Bishops and Executives of a number of southwest Pennsylvania Churches' to provide evidence of the strong religious support for organ donation as 'the gift of life' as follows :

> "God, as the greatest of his creative acts made human mankind in his own image and invested us with responsibility as stewards of life and creation. The gift of new life in Jesus Christ demonstrates further God's desire that human beings share the highest quality of life possible. We believe that organ donation and transplantation are not only in harmony with, but also reflect, the truths of creation and redemption. Christians, therefore, ought to pledge themselves, in appropriate circumstances and in accordance with their respective traditions and consciences to support and to participate in organ donation and transplantation" (Horton and Horton 1990; 798).

In a small scale interview study conducted by Exley et al. in Coventry (U.K.) among the members of the Sikh community, the representatives of the Gurudwaras stated "...as part of the Sikh religion is concerned with giving and helping others to the greatest extent possible, organ donation is an excellent way of exhibiting such altruism"[5] (1996; 25).

Sharp argues that the ethic of altruism is invoked in the 'gift' ideology to encourage the donors and recipients to accept organ donation as a selfless act of generosity that requires no reciprocity (1995; 375). Nevertheless, reciprocity is an important component of any gift exchange transaction. For, as Mauss, the famous French sociologist (in Sharp 1995; 379) noted:

> "In theory --- gifts are voluntary, yet, in fact, they are given and repaid under obligation. (Sharp 1995; 379).

In the context of organ transplantation, the obligation or the desire to reciprocate may be explained in terms of what Fox and Swazey call the 'tyranny of the gift' (in Gregory and Lonnquist 1996; 350). According to Fox and Swazey, when the donation of an organ occurs, a type of 'obligation to repay' is incurred by the recipient. Having received something so profoundly important, the recipient becomes in a sense, a debtor - owing something back to the donor. This is what they call the 'tyranny of the gift' (Gregory and Lonnquist 1996; 350). This can be compared to the Maussian concept of 'spiritual power of the gift' or the 'hau' among Maori people in Melanesia studied by Mauss. In the words of a Maori native, according to Mauss (1967; 11), the obligation to reciprocate the gifts was explained in the following words:

> "... Let us suppose that you possess a certain article (*toonga*) and that you give me this article. You give it me without setting a price on it. We strike no bargain about it. Now, I give this article to a third person who, after a certain lapse of time, decides to give me something as payment in return (*utu*). He makes a present to me of something (*toonga*). Now, this *toonga* that he gives me is the spirit (*hau*) of the *toonga* that I had received from you and that I had given to

5. This statement cannot be generalized because the validity of the data can be questioned and it is not supported by evidence such as sacred literature.

him. The *toonga* that I received for these *toonga* (which came from you) must be returned to you. It would not be fair (*tika*) on my part to keep these *toonga* for myself, whether they were desirable (*rawe*) or undesirable (*kino*). I must give them to you because they are *hau* of the *toonga* that you gave me. If I kept this other *toonga* for myself, serious harm might befall me, even death. This is the nature of the *hau*, the *hau* of personal property, the *hau* of the *toonga*, the *hau* of the forest ...." (Mauss 1967;11).

Thus, Maori people explain the obligation to reciprocate the gifts by the very fact that the gifts possess the spiritual 'hau' which exercises force on the recipient and tends to go back to the original giver. Therefore, the gifts must be reciprocated. The force of reciprocity is seen in the context of organ transplantation also. The symbolic weight of the organ drives the recipient to reciprocate. However, an organ cannot be reciprocated by another organ donation, as it happens in gift exchange among the Maoris. In a study conducted by Sharp in U.S.A., on the nature of exchange relationship between organ donors and recipients, many recipients expressed the desire for some form of equal and anonymous (indirect) exchange. Since transplant patients take immuno suppressants and powerful steroids, they cannot be organ donors when they die. Therefore, majority of the informants in Sharp's study chose to reciprocate by being active in human service programmes, either through their employment or as volunteers helping the elderly, single mothers, the poor and the homeless (1995; 375).

The obligation to reciprocate, however, springs up not just from the recipients side but the donor himself or his kin may expect to be reciprocated in some way. E.g. in a study conducted by Joralemon, Sylvia, a live transplant recipient immediately declared after her transplant that her donor expected to be compensated for the donated organ (1995 : 344). Thus, to describe organ donation as an extraordinary gift or as a 'gift of life' that cannot be reciprocated will be to disguise the inherent reciprocity that always underlies any transaction that we may call a gift transaction.

It is interesting to note that Mauss highlighted the element of reciprocity in not just the exchange that takes place between men but also in the exchange that takes place between men and Gods. This throws light on the whole aspect of the theory of sacrifice. According to Mauss, the sacrifice is intended to incite the spirit of the dead ancestors and the Gods to be generous towards them. The gifts given to Gods in the form of sacrifices serve the purpose of buying peace or to get rid of the evil spirits who enter into men and kill them. Since the sacrifice made to God and spirits is expected to be reciprocated by them, Mauss calls them 'contract sacrifices' which are intended to get a considerable thing in the place of a small one (1967; 100).

Mauss further extends the notion of 'contract sacrifices' to that of giving alms to the poor. In this case, the sacrifice is made not directly to God but to the poor for the sake of God because it is believed that Gods and spirits accept the idea that the share of wealth and happiness that has been given to the wealthy should serve the poor and children. For example, among the Hausa in Sudan, when the Guinea corn is ripe, fevers spread and the only way to avoid this fever, according to the natives, is to make presents of this grain to the poor because these gifts to children and the poor are pleasing to God. Since the sacrifice of grain is given indirectly to God, the reciprocity expected out of it is also indirect, that is, it is not expected from the poor or children to whom the grain is given but from God. Nevertheless, Mauss emphasizes that gift giving always entails reciprocity, whether between men or between men and Gods.

In the context of organ transplantation, Sharp argues that reciprocity is not a simple affair for the gift is simultaneously a thing and a person (1995; 379). Sharp further quotes Fox and Swazey as follows:

> "The psychological and moral burden of the gift is especially onerous because the gift ...is so extraordinary. It has no physical or symbolic equivalent. As a consequence, the giver, the receiver and their families may find.themselves locked in a creditor - debtor vise that binds them one to another in a mutually fettering way (Sharp 1995:365).

The unusual or the extraordinary nature of the gift of organ (the gift of life), thus, requires long term reciprocal obligations. As Mauss (in Ohunki-Tierney 1994; 241) indicated, "The return gift is a critical element in turning gift giving into gift exchange thereby creating social relationships among strangers". However, unlike any other exchange of commodities, Ohnuki-Tierney argues that organ donation cannot be called an organ exchange because the gift of an organ cannot be reciprocated by giving a similar organ or even a better or lesser organ (1994; 241). Therefore, the term suggested for addressing the act of giving organs is interchange, rather than 'exchange' because the term 'interchange' leaves scope for reciprocity but not of the same gift or from the same person to whom a gift (of organ) is given. Even though the gift of an organ is not reciprocated with a similar gift, it does facilitate the establishment of long term social relations between individuals and families.

The donor and his family may look forward to long term social relations with the recipient and his family because they believe that their lost relative is living in the recipient's body. Several scholars have described cases where donor's relatives are comforted to see and feel their deceased relative's organs having been transplanted in a recipient. Daar and Marshall argue that donating a deceased relative's organ gives the relatives a chance to salvage something good and hopeful out of a tragic situation beyond their control, besides fulfilling their desire to be close to deceased through his organs living in some other body (1998;

131). In a study conducted by Sque and Payne on the donor's motivations to give their organs, a respondent explained his decision to donate his deceased wife's organ by stating that his wife had intended to help other people after she died and that he supported his wife's decision to facilitate the retrieval of her organs (1996; 1363). To quote the respondent : "... I think G would like that because she did talk about having a card, only she never got around to having one and being a caring and sharing person that she was, we said, yeah we'll do that ... she would be more than pleased and proud that we did really" (Sque and Payne 1996; 1363). In the same article, several respondents expressed other altruistic reasons and motivations for making donation decisions about the organs of the deceased family members. One young wife explained her decision as an attempt to give meaning to her husband's life. She said that her husband never achieved anything in his life and this could be the biggest thing he could ever achieve she gave her final decision to remove her husband's organs from his dead body (Sque and Payne 1996; 1364). Sharp describes the case of two men - Bob (kidney donor) and Ray (kidney recipient) who have established long lasting ties by activating the bonds of kinship. After transplantation, these two men sought out one another, became pen pals and friends. They now consider themselves to be 'brothers'. Although they live on opposite ends of the country, they and their wives get together regularly for transplant events and joint vacations (1995; 375).

However, the social relationship between a donor (or his kin) and a recipient (or his kin) is not always so simple, easy and straight forward. The act of organ donation, according to Sharp, may even lead to serious conflicts between them if the donors (or their kin) continue to lay claim to the donated organs. To illustrate a strained social relationship between donor's kin and the recipient, Sharp cites the case of Ralph (double lung transplant recipient) and his donor's widow - Mary Rose. For three years, Ralph exchanged letters and Christmas cards with Mary Rose. In her letters and cards, Mary Rose informed Ralph of the circumstances of her husband's death, her pregnant state when her husband died, the subsequent birth of that child, her marriage to her former husband's best friend and the birth of another child. Despite its apparent closeness, the relationship is clouded with ambivalence because Ralph and Mary both interpret the nature of the gift differently (1995 : 376). As Ralph explains:

> "Her husband gave me two good lungs, it is my responsibility to get together sometime but I don't think I want to meet her, though she thinks that her husband lives on in me but I feel uncomfortable about that. I feel they are my lungs now. My job is to take care of them because he took such good care of them, too" (Sharp 1995; 376).

In the above case, the conflict between Ralph and Mary, according to Sharp, is due to their different perceptions of debt obligations involved in organ donation. Urged by the rhetoric of altruism, Mary Rose is comforted by the belief that her lost husband is still living by being embodied in those lungs that have been placed in Ralph. She perceives her husband's lungs as living on even though the body as a whole has been declared dead. She wants to maintain social links with her husband through these lungs and therefore attempts to exert control over Ralph by dwelling upon the ties of kinship. Ralph, in contrast, struggles to maintain a unique personal identity while simultaneously feeling the need to reciprocate. He views himself not so much as Mary's deceased husband but as the new caretaker of those lungs that now breathe in his chest. He wishes to form his own biography in private without interference from Mary and expects her to be simply a generous stranger who has given willingly and selflessly and whose actions are driven by kindness and love (1995; 376).

To avoid such conflicts between the donor and recipient

as seen between Ralph and Mary Rose, the transplant professionals often hide the identity of the donor from the recipient and vice versa. Bavinck informs that the name and the identity of the donor is kept secret and confidential from the recipient because of the danger that "this knowledge will become a psychological burden to the recipient, to such an extent that it could interfere with the process of his recovery" (1996; 82). One reason for maintaining an anonymity of the identities of the donor and the recipient, according to an editorial in the Lancet, is that when an organ has been given freely, regret about a decision can follow. For example, when families of somebody who has been killed by a drunk driver learn that the organ recipient is an alcoholic, their pain and possibly disappointment are not hard to imagine. Therefore, the editorial suggests that the principle of confidentiality about who donors or recipients are should be adhered to (March 4, 2000; 765).

Sharp observed at Mercy Memorial Hospital in the U.S. that the "transplant professionals follow a strict protocol that dictates what sort of information should be withheld from recipients. For example, prior to transplantation, a patient is only told of the organ and is not provided with any description of the donor. Following surgery, the recipient is informed about the age, sex, marital status and sometimes the race of the donor. The recipient may also be given a vague description of how that donor died and from what general area of the state or the nation he or she came. A recipient is not given the donor's name or address. Similarly, only certain types of death are reported: automobile and motorcycle accidents (because of their accidental nature) are viewed as the most acceptable narratives. Circumstances involving suicide or murder, however, are not mentioned. Occasionally, a donor's personal or social history may also be 'doctored'. For example, one health professional at the Transplant Games reported a case in which a pimp was described as a family man" (1995; 368-369).

An important point to be noted here is that if anonymity is emphasized and the donors and recipients are prevented from knowing each other, then, how does the 'gift' ideology maintain its characterizing feature, that is, the development of a long term relationship? According to Ohnuki-Tierney, the absence of a social relationship between the donor and receiver, thus, questions the applicability of the 'gift' ideology to organ donation because it is the establishment and maintenance of human relationships that distinguishes a gift from a commodity. According to her, "whether between individuals or between social groups, gift exchange facilitates inter dependency among individuals in transaction, in contrast to commodity transactions which take place between independent individuals without social ties" (1994; 241).

The 'gift' giving paradigm, therefore, does not seem to be an adequate ideological strategy to support organ donation. While the public has largely positive views about the 'gift' ideology towards organ donation, Skumanich and Kinstfather argue that this sentiment has not led to the subsequent behavioral commitment in the form of signed organ donor cards.[6] Although, the U.S. has the highest rate of awareness regarding organ donation, it is estimated that only 14% of the U.S. population carry signed organ donor cards (1996 : 401). According to Ohnuki-Tierney, "it is extremely dangerous to cloak organ donation in gift wrapping" (1994; 241). It does not seem to be a practical strategy either because it obscures the ways in which the decisions are made at the level of practice, e.g., who makes the decision to donate the organ - the donor or his kin? The 'gift' ideologists' claim to morality and altruism has also been challenged by the advocates of the 'market' ideology.

---

6. Organ donor card is a legal document signed by an individual in front of two witnesses who are his family members, giving his consent for the removal of organs after his death (including brain death) (Skumanich and Kintsfather 1996; 401).

The Market Ideology

Challenging the claims and arguments of the 'gift' ideologists, the proponents of the 'market' ideology argue that body organs should be treated like any other commodity and as one's private property. That is why it is also called the 'property rights' ideology. The basic contention of the 'market' ideologists is that individuals should be free to sell their body parts as they would sell any other commodity owned by them.

Rothman questions - "why ban the sale of kidneys when the sale of other body parts including semen, female eggs, hair and blood is allowed in many countries? ...transplant surgeons, nurses and social workers as well as transplant retrieval teams and the hospitals are all paid for their work? Why should only the donor and the donor's family go without compensation?" (1998; 15). Taking the 'market' ideology to its extreme, Rothman argues that refusing the poor sellers (owners of organs), a chance to make the money they desperately need, would be an unjustifiable form of paternalism (1998; 15). Answering the critics who argue that the sellers may be at a greater risk living with one kidney, he states that studies do not show any significant differences in health among donor and non-donor siblings. He supports this view by citing a study conducted at the university of Minnesota where a comparison was made between 78 kidney donors with their non donor siblings after twenty years and which showed no significant differences in their health (Rothman 1998; 15). Rothman adds, "Even the risk conscious insurance companies do not raise their rates (premium) for kidney donors" (1998; 15).

Supporting the 'market' ideology, Joralemon argues that since a corpse is considered to be the property of the next of kin in so far as he on she has the right and obligation to claim it for burial, then why can't living individuals be permitted full property rights over their own bodies to do whatever they wish with it (including sales of organs) (1995; 340).

The 'market' ideologists do not accept that an individual could give a part of his body without any financial incentive. Mere altruism, they argue, is not a reason sufficient enough to motivate an individual to give his body organ either to a relative or to a stranger. This ideological stand is supported by several statements made by leading doctors in India to the press. As Vij and Kalghatgi reported, "Doctor Vatsala Trivedi[7] refuses to believe that any individual would donate a part of his body to a stranger unless a financial consideration is involved" (1998). In a similar vein, Doctor D.S. Rana[8] stated, "In fact, even relatives charge money for a donation. A young man who has donated a kidney to his elder brother might take a share of the business but the family allows it as the money remains within the family" (The Times of India, Delhi, August 13, 2000).

According to Vij and Kalghatgi (1998), each month doctors at the All India Institute of Medical Sciences, New Delhi, receive atleast a dozen letters from people desperate to donate a kidney for a price. In one of these letters, a 22 year old Mukhtar Ahmad Sheikh from Srinagar (whose family business was wiped out by terrorists) wrote:

> "... I can only think of 3 ways of ending my family's problems. First to kill my conscience and become a terrorist. Second, to kill myself, that is, commit suicide and leave my family to their fate or third, to sell my kidney to anyone who is in utmost need for it.
>
> One of my friends, a medical student, told me about this solution. I thought this act will not only save me from becoming a merciless terrorist but also save a valuable life...

---

7. Doctor Vatsala Trivedi is a urologist at Sion Hospital, Mumbai, India who performed the first cadaver transplant in Maharashtra (Vij and Kalghatgi; 1998).
8. Doctor D.S. Rana is a Chief Nephrologist at Sir Ganga Ram Hospital, New Dehli, India.

After God, you, Sir, are my last hope. Please save me, my family and also another life. You will save me from getting into the hell of terrorism and save my own country. (Excerpts from the letter to the Head of the Nephrology department, All India Institute of Medical Sciences, New Delhi) (Vij and Kalghatgi : 1998).

The above, clearly supports and defends the 'market' ideology.

The 'market' ideology is often criticized as being unethical and exploitative because of its rendering of body parts as commodities. However, the advocates of 'market' ideology argue that denying a poor person a chance to earn a decent living by selling his own body part would be highly unethical. Doctor Nundy[9] says, "If you talk to potential donors, they say that they need the money to start a business or to get their daughter married" (Vij and Kalghatgi 1998). Similarly, Doctor Vijay Kher[10] states, "I have seen that the majority of donors are... financially disadvantaged... And I won't be surprised if money changes hands within the family" (Vij and Kalghatgi 1998). 'Hindustan Times' also reports, "Almost all donors are poor labourers or industrial workers" (December, 10, 2000).

Thus, the 'market' ideology can be defended on its own ethical grounds. According to its advocates, saving a life is more important than maintaining such principles of altruism, generosity, selflessness, humanitarianism etc. If, in this process, a poor helpless donor gets a financial compensation (as in the case of Mukhtar Ahmad Sheikh mentioned above), then two lives will be saved in one instance which is highly ethical. Doctor Amit Kumar who was arrested by the Delhi Police for his alleged involvement in a kidney

9. Doctor S. Nundy is at Sir Ganga Ram Hospital, New Delhi.
10. Doctor Vijay Kher is the Head of the Nephrology at Indraprastha Apollo Hospital, New Delhi.

trade, defended his position by arguing that he was providing a helping hand for his patients. As he stated, "I was helping out people by performing these operations as it is difficult to live with two damaged kidneys. The transplants gave them a new life. It helped the donors as well" (Hindustan Times, December 10, 2000, New Delhi). Perry also argues, "it is immoral to waste transplantable human organs during a period of scarcity which results in human suffering and death (1981; 165).

The way in which the 'market' ideology is gaining popularity among transplant professionals, donors and recipients is evident from the language used by them to refer to transplantable organs in their discussions about organ shortage. For example, Sharp observed at Mercy Memorial Hospital in the U.S.A. that the language used by the recipients when they assembled together revealed their ability to objectify organs. For instance, they discussed the shortage of organs as though they were spare parts for valuable cars (1995; 370). Referring to the commodification of kidneys, Doctor Vatsala Trivedi states, "It is just like the car market. The products are expensive as long as the demand is less and the availability is low" (Vij and Kalghatgi 1998). 'The Times of India' also reported, "the kidneys, it seems, are worth their weight in gold" (December 7, 2000). Similarly, reporting on the selling of kidneys, 'Hindustan Times' mentioned, 'Setting up a kidney shop' (December 10, 2000, Delhi). Supporting the 'market' ideology, Benoist and Cathebras quote Descartes as considering himself " primarily as having a face, hands, arms... bones and flesh... Like a clock composed of counter weights..." (1993; 861).

Such an objectification and depersonalization of body parts is nothing but an ambiguous way of presenting facts and interpreting reality because in every society and culture,human body and its parts are open to symbolic interpretation. For example, in the American society, as Sharp states, the heart is generally conceived of as the seat of love and passion. It is the self or the soul while the brain is associated with rationality and consciousness. Lungs, on the other hand, are represented as the breadth of life (1995; 372). It follows that to translate market ideology into practice, the body organs will have to be divested from such metaphorical frills.

The basic concern of the 'market' ideology is to increase the availability of organs for transplantation. For this, they argue, a mere altruistic motive is insufficient to generate the required number of organs. A financial incentive, on the other hand, would not only motivate the living persons to donate kidneys but also motivate the families of the dead to donate organs of the deceased, who would otherwise be unwilling to take an immediate decision at the grieving moment of their relative's death. According to Obermann, "economists argue that a price for blood would raise the blood supply as those who donate would be even happier to do so and those who are reluctant to donate may be persuaded by the financial incentives" (1997; 302). Joralemon argues that the faith of the 'market' ideologists rests in the potential of the markets to provide incentives that would balance the supply and demand of organs. As he puts it, "The proponents of the property rights ideology believe that the rising shortage of donors would eventually force the application of market principles of supply and demand to organ procurement. Thus, the cultural priorities invoked by 'market' ideologists are individual autonomy and rational self interest" (Joralemon 1995; 344). Obermann seems to be supporting this view when he states that "the considerations behind financial incentives in organ donation are based on the notion of a rational, self interested, welfare maximizing individual, weighing the losses and benefits incremented on him or her by a specific behaviour" (1997; 302).

Whereas a financial incentive might increase the availability of organs by increasing the level of motivation among donors, it might even have a negative affect on organ availability if organs are commodified to the extent of exploiting the donors.

For example, if organs are taken from patients without their approval or if the major share of money is taken by the touts, brokers or middlemen who arrange the deal between the donors and recipients. The doctors at the All India Institute of Medical Sciences, New Delhi, as reported in 'Hindustan Times' (December 10, 2000) said that "the price of each kidney varies from Rs. 40,000 to Rs. 1 lakh depending upon how the broker and the donor can negotiate".

The commodification of organs might even result in a black market in organs. According to Bavinck, "Trading in human organs can lead to scenarios which include murder and blackmail". He says that where money is the main objective things can easily be manipulated. After all, he questions, how can one be sure that the tissue matching of the donor and the recipient have been carried out correctly? Matching costs both time and money and dealers have no interest in a good match between donor and recipient. They simply want to make as much money as possible and as quickly as possible (1996; 83). Describing the flourishing black market in organs in Mumbai, Rothman informs, "The sellers in these markets include impoverished villagers, slum dwellers, power room operators and manual laborers. The buyers, on the other hand, come from Egypt, Kuwait, Oman and other Gulf states and from India's enormous middle class (which numbers atleast 200 million). They readily pay between $2,500 and $4,000 of which the donors, if he is not cheated, receives between $1,000 and $1,500. The rest goes to the touts (1998; 115). The touts and brokers, according to Rothman, defend the growing markets in organs by taking the moral plea that they bring together the desperately poor with the desperately ill" (1998; 15).

Criticizing the 'market' ideology, Rothman argues, "just because some body parts have already been turned into commodities does not mean that an increasing trade in kidneys and other organs is desirable. Many of the poor Indians who sell their organs clearly feel that they have had to submit to a painful experience and a degrading practice in order to get badly needed sums of money" (1998; 15). According to Gregory and Lonnquist, "the critics of the strong market approach worry that the financial incentives may place undue pressure on low income persons and people in the third world to donate. Once organs are on the market, the wealthy clearly would have easier access" (1996; 349). Joralemon also argues that "despite all the reasoned arguments and moral insistence by the market advocates, most donors do not like to equate their body parts with the property they buy and sell" (1995, 348). Obermann states that "monetary incentives may... destroy an existing sense of commitment... financial rewards may even reduce one's inclination to donate organs" (1997;302). He further states that "Monetising the action of giving a 'gift of life' can be taken as highly insulting and some who in principle are willing to donate would actually refuse to provide an organ in this instance" (Obermann 1997; 303).

Low also argues that "the commoditization of body parts for financial rewards creates a world where cultural practices are violated in order to serve the financial and technological demands of medical institutions" (1994; 477). According to Sharp, "the medical ethicists, on their part, are demanding moral parameters for the use of human body parts. Their common concern is that medical technological advances are outpacing ethical discussion by ignoring the collective beliefs and experiences of the patients" (1995; 359). Joralemon states that "the increasing acceptance of market ideology in transplantation has also led to the cross cultural suspicion that commodification of body parts may stimulate 'unacceptable violations of human rights' which is evident in the proliferation of sensational stories of black markets in organs". An unfortunate consequence of such a story, according to Joralemon, was "the savage beating on March 29, 1993 of June Weinstock, an Alaskan environmentalist accused by an angry crowd of stealing a child for procuring his body parts during a visit to San Cristobal" (1995; 341).

The 'market' ideology, thus, suffers on ethical and moral grounds. It is confronted with cultural resistance and therefore, does not seem to be an acceptable organ procurement strategy to a vast majority of people. This is evident in the widespread resistance to commodification of body parts expressed in newspapers, magazines, journals and academic literature. In popular discussions, too, the 'market' ideology towards procurement of organs invites the anger of people and is generally the subject of criticism.

The Solution

Both the 'gift' as well as the 'market' procurement strategies appear to be ineffective in the supply of an adequate number of organs for transplantation commensurate with the need. However, Joralemon argues, "both the proposals have gained enough acceptance to be the subject of debate rather than of dismissal" (1995; 346). According to Perry, "The trouble... is to design a policy which might actually be effective in eliminating suffering and death for need of a transplantable organ and yet not violate any moral principle..." (1981; 163). Thus, there is an urgent need for a middle position that would combine the benefits of both the 'market' and the 'gift' ideologies.

The middle position between the 'gift' and the 'market' ideologies has been taken by several scholars and professionals. E.G. Lock argues that "neither a model of altruism nor one in which a dead body is understood simply as an aggregation of body parts is sufficient to meet the growing demand of transplantable organs" (1995; 392). Similarly Daar and Marshall argue that there is a border area between donation and sale of organs which they call the 'grey basket'. The middle path, according to them, "is actually a culturally acceptable form of paid donation such as the one adopted by Doctor Reddy and his colleagues in Chennai wherein middle men were eliminated, donors were selected after psychological evaluation, fixed payments were made transparent, advice was given on investing the money and donors were insured for sickness benefits for 3 years after donation" (1998; 128).

Davis argues for two policies worth considering as a mid-way solution between 'gift' and 'market' ideologies, namely, 'mandated choice' and 'presumed consent'. 'Mandated choice', according to him, "requires people to say whether or not they will donate their organs when they renew a driver's license, file an income tax form, or perform some other task required by the state". Donor consent, according to him, would be indicated on the driver's license or in a state donor register accessible at the time of death. This approach, he argues, "allows consent to be expressed in advance of illness and death, thus, promoting individual autonomy by allowing competent adults to make the donation decision for themselves rather than leaving it to the relatives to decide" (1999; 1382). Under 'presumed consent', Davis argues, "people are assumed to consent to be cadaveric organ donors unless they or their families explicitly refuse to donate" (1990; 1383). Supporting this view, Berry suggests that "it is time for the U.S. to consider the policy of 'presumed consent' where people are presumed to have consented to donating their organs when they die unless they proactively opt out" (1999; 1445).

Another proponent of the middle position is Schubert who argues that both the altruistic as well as the reimbursement oriented giving must be encouraged in blood donations. As he states, "... the door to a mixed system of voluntary and commercial blood must always remain open... the best approach is professionalism regardless of which ideological approach it advances" (1994; 201). Schubert believes that it is too simplistic to reduce the problem to voluntary versus commercial blood collection systems as if it is a battle between ethics and economics. In reality, both voluntary and competitive blood collection systems are prone to inefficiencies and inequalities, therefore, both must be regulated to cope with the problem of scarcity and, thus, ensure a sufficient and optimal supply of blood (1994; 201). In a similar vein, Bavinck seems to argue for some kind of commercial mediation centre to be set up that would acquire organs and make them available at a cost price (1996; 83).

The mid way solution between the 'gift' and the 'market' ideologies is a recently devised organ procurement strategy which is still in a state of infancy. The idea is to promote altruism and provide compensation and, thus, increase the supply of organs for transplantation. As Perry argues, the purpose of propagating a middle solution between gift and market ideologies is to reduce needless human suffering and to do so at no one's expense (1981; 163). Doctor S.K. Aggarwal, Nephrologist, All India Institute of Medical Sciences, also argues, "You cannot deny the renal failure patient the right to live and at the same time the poor cannot be exploited in an inhuman manner" (Hindustan Times, Delhi, December, 10, 2000). However, it must be remembered that it is only when such policies are enacted with state and pubic approval that their real efficacy towards procurement of organs can be judged or evaluated.

4

LEGAL ISSUES AND ENACTMENTS

We have already seen that the medical therapy of organ transplantation has implications far beyond the medical sphere, extending into the socio-religious, economic and cultural domains. We will now see that the legal sphere is another important and crucial domain in every society where socio-cultural norms, beliefs and practices related to organ transplantation get codified and structured within the framework of rules and regulations. The legal regulation of transplantation is an important tool in the development of transplant techniques - facilitating or constraining it through the regulation of organ procurement and their utilization procedures.

In the examination of organ access and procurement legislations in some countries (The United States, Sweden, China, Italy, Great Britain and India), an attempt is made to raise issues such as the accepted and prescribed form of organ donation, medico-economic causes as well as socio-cultural implications of transplant legislations across nations. Machado argues that examining law in the socio-cultural context entails studying law as a cultural symbol and as a powerful guideline in defining social reality. In regulating the uses of human organs and tissues, he states that transplant enactments encode socio-cultural assumptions, concepts and beliefs concerning the body and body parts. This is expressed in the outline of boundaries and rules for the transfer of body parts, that is, the regulation of social actions such as giving (in this context defined as donation) and receiving (1996; 159). According to Machado, an organ transplant legislation makes a significant contribution in shaping what forms of giving and receiving are to be socially and culturally permissible, required or forbidden (1996; 159). Following Machado's argument, we examine below various organ transplant legislations in their socio-cultural contexts.

As mentioned in the previous chapter, culturally evoked normative controversy between the 'gift' and 'market' paradigms is actually a controversy between the 2 basic ideologies - altruism and commodification (property rights). Gregory and Lonnquist suggest five alternatives that are available to a country to enact and formulate an organ donation policy or legislation[1]. As we shall examine below, these alternatives are consistent with either of these two cultural norms. The 5 organ donation policy options as given by Gregory and Lonnquist are (1998; 348) :

* **Strong Required Request:** Every citizen would be asked to indicate his or her willingness to participate in organ donation — either on income tax returns or through a mandatory check off on the driver's license. This policy retains the voluntaristic / altruistic nature of the system but is more aggressive in forcing people to consider organ donation and to take a formal position.

Since the policy encourages altruism among donors, it is consistent with the 'gift' ideology. Altruism may be of two kinds. First is the altruism which is inter-personal in nature and takes place between individuals (this is typically the Maussian concept of altruism; 1967). Second is the generalized and anonymous altruism which does not involve inter-personal transactions.

1. It may be noted that these are ideal typical categories and that the transplant laws of different countries do not conform to them exactly. The law may, in fact, combine some characteristics of different policies.

* **Weak Presumed Consent:** Hospitals would be required by law to remove and use all suitable cadaver organs for donation unless the deceased had expressly objected through a central registry or a non-donor card or family members objected.

This policy also maintains an altruistic purpose but presumes that donation will occur unless there is a deliberate objection to it. This policy is also consistent with the 'gift' ideology.

* **Strong Presumed Consent:** Physicians would be given complete authorization to remove usable organs regardless of the wishes of the deceased or family members. It is the only alternative that eliminates the voluntary dimension of organ donation policy but it is also the policy that retrieves the largest number of transplantable organs.

This policy is consistent neither with the 'altruistic' nor with the 'market' cultural ideologies but is rather representative of the middle position between them.

* **Weak Market Approach:** Individuals or next-of-kin for deceased donors would receive a tax benefit for the donation of organs (perhaps a one-year deduction from federal and state taxes) or a cash payment of sufficient size to offset some funeral expenses. This approach adds financial incentive to the act of donation, thus eliminating the role of altruism.

This policy is, therefore, consistent with the 'market' ideology.

* **Strong Market Approach:** The individuals or next-of-kin would be able to auction organs to the highest bidder. Like the Weak Market Approach, this system places greater emphasis on increasing the number of organs donated than on retaining altruistic motivation for donation.

This policy is consistent with the 'market' ideology.

Let us now study the particular transplant legislations in different countries in detail :

The United States

The United States legally addressed the question of organ procurement in 1968 by passing the first federal legislative enactment on organ donation called the Uniform Anatomical Gift Act (Joralemon 1995; 343). As it is clear from the title (which addresses organ donation as gift giving), the U.S. legislation encouraged the attitude of altruism, generosity and helpfulness in the donation of organs. By making the donation of organs legal, as Gregory and Lonnquist argue, it was hoped that the volunteers would come forward. The courts ruled that competent adults could voluntarily donate organs to relatives which, at first, seemed like the only possibility. Organs could also be donated by minors but only with parental and judicial consent (1996; 347).

As a result of the passing of this Act, Gregory and Lonnquist argue that donation of organs did increase but as the supply was increasing so was the demand. By 1971, this Act was adopted in every state in the United States. The Act now permitted adults to donate the whole or part of their body after death through donor cards and living wills and gave next of kin authority to donate after an individual's death as long as no contrary instructions had been given. The Act according to Gregory and Lonnquist "maintained the country's allegiance to a voluntaristic and altruistic approach and was successful in increasing the number of donors" (1996; 347).

However, according to Gregory and Lonnquist, about 90% of the 20,000 - 25,000 people who were potential donors each year in the United States still failed to donate because there was no centralized system for identifying and locating those who needed organ donation and those who were willing to make a donation.

According to them, a dramatic change in organ donation policy occurred in 1987 with greater emphasis on the 'Weak Required Request Policy'. Consequently, in order to receive essential medicare and medicaid reimbursements, the hospitals in the U.S. were required to make patients and their families aware of the organ donation option and notify a federally certified Organ Procurement Agency (OPA) when there was a consent to donation (1996; 348).

Gregory and Lonnquist conclude that the passage of the Uniform Anatomical Gift Act has certainly increased the number of organ donations in the United States. According to them, in 1991, out of 6,759 organ donors, about two thirds were cadavers and they contributed approximately 16,000 transplantable organs. Nevertheless, in 1995, there were still more than 30,000 people on the waiting lists in Richmond itself who had been medically and financially approved for transplants. However, they estimate that about one-third of the people on the waiting list will die before receiving a transplant (1996; 348).

An analysis of the Weak Required Request Policy in the United States, according to Gregory and Lonnquist, reveals that the Act maintains the voluntaristic and altruistic nature of gift giving in organ donation but seeks to ensure that potential donors are aware of the donation option (1996; 348).

Sweden

In Sweden, according to Machado, the first act to regulate organ transplantation was promulgated in 1958 under the rubric 'Act on the Use of Tissue and Other Biological Material'. It regulated the use of corpses for purposes of transplantation. Machado states that the organ procurement policy applied was of 'presumed consent'. Organ or tissue extraction could be performed if the potential donor or the next of kin did not explicitly refuse the procedure or if there were no grounds to believe that they would refuse. Informing the next of kin was not mandatory (1996; 160).

In the Act of 1975, Machado informs, rule of 'presumed consent' was left unchanged but some amendments were introduced. The next of kin were to be informed prior to the procedure, if possible. If no close relative was available, the physician was permitted to perform the organ extraction. Nevertheless, for the extraction of organs for transplantation from living donors, written consent was established as mandatory. If these living donors were not legally competent (e.g. minors and mentally handicapped), the authorization of the board of health was required (1996; 160).

Until 1987, according to Machado, physicians in the hospitals in Sweden were authorized by the state to remove transplantable organs for purposes of transplantation from deceased persons unless they had explicitly indicated their opposition to this. The issue of 'presumed consent' regarding the extraction of organs and tissues for transplantation, thereafter, became subject to serious debates which led to the amendment of the 1975 transplant Act. The amendment resulted in the replacement of the notion of 'presumed consent' by that of 'presumed non-consent' in the case of dead donors in 1987. Accordingly, if no previous written authorization by the deceased was available, the cons nt of the deceased was presumed to be negative and, therefore, organ extraction was not permissible unless the next of kin as representatives of the deceased authorized the extraction. In constituting the next of kin as representatives of the will of the deceased, Machado points out, the state resurrected the traditional kin rights (1996; 161).

An important point to be noted in the context of Swedish transplant legislation, as stated by Machado, is that neither donor nor family can determine the donee, physician or institution that will finally receive the organs or tissues. Moreover, the act of giving or donating, although not explicitly defined in the text of the Act, is discussed as 'the unselfish act of giving' in the preparatory texts (1996; 160-161).

Thus, the motivating ideology recognized by Sweden to procure organs for transplantation from its people is that of the 'gift' or 'altruism'. Clearly, the 'commodity' ideology is rejected in the Swedish legislation on organ procurement and transplantation since anonymity is maintained between the donor and the recipient. Therefore, money cannot be directly exchanged in the transfer of organs. Even if the Swedish policy of 'presumed consent' of 1857 is considered, it should be noted that the legislation did not permit the physicians or the state to commodify or sell the organs as the act of donation is represented as 'the unselfish act of giving'. Hence, it can be said that the Swedish transplant legislation conforms to the cultural ideology of 'altruism'.

Italy

In Italy, the legislation of organ procurement and use for transplantation is divided into 2 parts from living donors and from cadaveric donors. According to Wolstenholme and O'Connor, In July 1965 a Bill No. 1321 called 'Kidney Transplantation from Living Donors' was passed in Italy which allowed for kidney donations from a live donor for transplantation only when the donation is from an adult person and is supported by donor's written consent. The two authors state that the donation comprises a written declaration on plain paper showing the donor's free and determined will to make such a donation. The donation is, however, not accepted by the state if it contains any condition concerning the mode of disposition or if deficiency of the donor's free will is clearly proved (1996; 178-179).

The Italian law, according to Fluss, is evidently the first to address the issue of commerce in organs for transplantation. It prohibits any form of award or compensation for living kidney donors (1991; 307). Wolstenholme and O'Connor seem to be supporting this claim by Fluss when they cite Article 8 of the Act according to which, "any kidney donation is to be void when money compensation or other utility is agreed". Also, according to Article 9, as cited by them, "whoever works as a middleman in kidney donation for the sake of money will be sentenced to imprisonment from 3 months to one year and fined 100,000 to 2 million Lira" (1996;182).

In September, 1965 an Act no. 1156 called 'Kidney Transplantation from Cadaver Donors' was passed in Italy which allowed for the removal of body parts of a cadaver. According to Wolstenholme and O'Connor, the provisions of the Act authorized the district physicians to remove the organs of a cadaver only after the presentation of a testamentary disposition which contains the manifest will of the dead person stating that parts from his body may be removed for transplantation purposes. If the testamentary disposition is missing, the hospital physician must contact the husband or wife of the deceased or his relatives to the second degree of whom the address is known. The removal, however, is not allowed if it is opposed in time by the husband or the wife of the deceased or by his relatives to the second degree (1996; 177-178).

It is clear from the above that the consent of the deceased (prior to his death) or his relative to the second degree is an important requirement in Italy for the medico-provinciale to be authorized to remove organs from a cadaver. It could be said that the Italian law by rejecting all sorts of compensation in cash or in kind, rejects the 'market' ideology. However, due to the strong intervention by the state in the act of organ extraction, the ideology of 'generalized altruism' takes precedence and importance in the Italian law as is the case with the Swedish law on organ donation.

Great Britain

In Great Britain, the use of parts of bodies of deceased persons for medical use is governed by the 'Human Tissues Act of 1961'. According to Calne, under the provisions of the Act, if any person, either in writing at any time or orally in the presence of two or more witnesses during his last illness expressed a request that his body or any specified part of his body be used after his death for transplantation or for purposes of medical education or research, the person lawfully in possession of his body after his death may authorize the removal of any or the specified part from his body. However, the act also authorizes the person lawfully in possession of the body of the deceased person to give his approval regarding the removal of parts from the dead body unless the deceased (prior to his death) or the surviving spouse had expressed an objection to his body being so dealt with after his death (1971; 184).

Calne states that in the absence of the permission having been given for organ removal by the dead person during his or her lifetime, the permission of the nearest relative must be sought before organ removal is carried out. This applies to the majority of prospective donors whose wishes are not known to the practitioner who certifies death. The possible exceptions to this are the occasions when sudden death occurs and the death certificate cannot immediately be issued. Under these circumstances, if every attempt to contact the relatives are unsuccessful, the transplant team is permitted to carry out the removal of organs before an irreversible damage occurs (1971; 184).

The transplant Act in Great Britain, therefore, relies on the policy of 'Weak Presumed Consent' since the requirement of consent of the deceased (prior to his death) or that of his kin in the form of a formal written legal document is not a mandatory criterion to authorize organ extraction. The oral consent of either the deceased or his kin is sufficient to legitimize the act of organ extraction from his body after death. Even in the absence of his consent, it is presumed to be there (in the case of accidents) unless objected to by him or his kin. It could, thus, be said that the ideology that underlies such a legislation is undoubtedly that of 'selfless' and 'generous altruism'.

China

China has reportedly adopted the tactic of harvesting the organs of executed prisoners (Rothman 1994; 15). According to Ikels, "In late 1984 rules affecting the specific issue of organ retrieval from executed criminals were issued in China jointly by the Supreme People's Court, Supreme People's Procuracy, Ministry of Public Security, Ministry of Justice, Ministry of Health and Ministry of Civil Affairs. These rules (Temporary Rules Concerning the Utilization of Corpses or Organs From the Corpses of Executed Criminals) reiterated that the corpses or organs of executed criminals could be utilized if no one claimed the body, the criminal had volunteered to donate or the family consented to the use of the corpse" (1997; 1278).

This Chinese practice of obtaining organs for transplantation from prisoners evoked sharp criticism by the international community, according to Ikels (1997; 1271). According to Rothman, this Chinese legislation allowing the utilization of organs from bodies of executed prisoners without their permission prior to death is officially treated as a state secret as it is clear from the following stipulations in the Act related to organ transplantation in China : "The use of corpses or organs of executed prisoners must be kept strictly secret and attention must be paid to avoid negative repercussions... the cars used to retrieve organs from the execution grounds should not bear health department insignia and the people involved in obtaining organs should not wear white uniforms" (1998; 15).

Since the above mentioned Chinese practice is kept confidential, Ikels informs that divulging information about it has resulted in legal and other sanctions. He cites the example of a former Chinese citizen Harry Wu who was arrested at the Chinese border in June 1995 and charged with 'stealing state secrets' in the course of his under cover research on this topic (1997; 1271). In the published works on organ procurement, Ikels notes that the Chinese authors usually refer to donors as victims of acute brain trauma as well as traffic accidents, suicides etc. and not to executions directly (1997; 1271).

According to Rothman, the system of organ procurement works very efficiently in China and the patients do not have to wait for long to get an organ (1998;16). As he informs, "Immediately before the execution, the physician sedates the prisoner and then inserts both a breathing tube in his lungs and a catheter in one of his veins. The prisoner is then executed with a bullet to his head; The physician immediately moves to stem the blood flow, attach a respirator to the breathing tube and inject drugs into the catheter so as to increase blood pressure and cardiac output. With the organs thus maintained, the body is transported to a hospital where the donor is waiting and the surgery is performed" (Rothman1998; 16). According to Rothman, "Executions can be timed to meet market needs and the supply is more than adequate" (1998;16). He describes the case of an American heart transplant surgeon, who was invited to China to perform a transplant. Accustomed to long waiting periods in America, the surgeon wanted to be sure that the heart would be available when he arrived. His would be hosts told him that they would schedule an execution to fit with his travel schedule (Rothman 1998; 16). Ikels reports two types of objections to the idea of obtaining organs for transplantation from executed prisoners. The first relates to the concept of capital punishment itself. Second relates to the impossibility of obtaining organs from individuals who are imprisoned in local jails in China (1997; 1280). Rothman voices his objection by stating that there is no way of ensuring that the court verdicts will not be influenced by the need for organs (1998; 16). However, according to Ikels, none of the objections is particularly persuasive to the members of the transplant community or the general public in China (1997; 1280). According to Rothman, China's system has its own defenders. The arguments used in their defense are : Why deprive prisoners of the opportunity to do a final act of goodness? If a person has a long criminal record, why not condemn him to death so that a worthy citizen might live? (1998; 16). As such, very few people in China, according to Ikels, are opposed to capital punishment for what are perceived as real criminals (e.g. murderers, rapists, serial robbers, bandits, kidnappers and the like). Nor do people view being in a prison as uniquely coercive. The individual is, infact, expected to acknowledge that the interests of the family, work place and the state should take priority over his or her own (1997; 1280).

Even though the Chinese are repeatedly charged with 'inhuman conduct' and being forced to discontinue their provision of taking organs from executed prisoners, Ikels says that it could still be argued that there is no real shortage of organs in China. Infact, there is a surplus and it is this surplus that makes possible transplantation to foreigners (Ikels 1997; 1282). Quoting a statement made by Zhang, a social researcher, Ikels remarks, "More than 10 years have passed since the issuing of the temporary rules but today the development of China's organ transplantation still depends on the corpses of criminals sentenced to death as the major source, even the sole source of supply of transplant organs which cannot but cause one to feel regret" (1997; 1279).

On the basis of the above discussion, it could be said that the Chinese legislation relies on the policy of 'Strong Presumed Consent' and is, therefore, consistent neither with the altruistic nor with the commodification ideologies. However, strong evidence reveals that Chinese officials profitably market the organs of their prisoners, largely because of the surplus availability of organs in China.

Ikels argues that the Chinese are more or less able to meet their demand of organs because of the policy of obtaining organs from the bodies of executed prisoners (1997;1282). However, this can be questioned. One may ask - are there sufficient executions performed in China so as to meet the demand of organs? Since the number of executions performed in China are kept strictly confidential, the validity of the statement which says that the corpses of executed prisoners meets up the demand of organs, is open to doubt and will continue to be so until there is reliable information about the number of organs required for transplantation and number of organs available from bodies of executed prisoners so that a sound comparison is made of both figures.

India

In India, in view of the illegal trading practices around organ procurement, particularly kidneys, the parliament passed 'The Transplantation of Human Organs Act 1994'. Amalorpavaṇathan describes the country's scenario of kidney trade before the passage of this legal enactment in 1994. According to him, the conditions were such that a poor man was willing to sell his kidney to combat poverty. This led to the rise of the most nefarious trade in India - 'The kidney trade' so much so that India came to be known internationally as the kidney bazaar with Mumbai and Chennai as major centres (1995; 611). According to Amalorpavanathan, one locality in Chennai - Villivakam came to be known as 'Kidney wakkam' (Bazaar) because the majority of residents of this area were forced by their poverty to eke out their living by selling their kidneys. As he informs, the kidney bazaar operated in such a way that a rich Arab with renal failure landed in one of the dubious nursing homes in Mumbai. A poor migrant labourer from Dharavi was encouraged to donate one of his kidneys for a sum of about Rs. 25,000. Thus, around Rs. 6 to 10 lakh would change hands in the entire deal with some hospitals doing 30 to 40 such operations a month (1995; 611). Amalorpavanathan argues that these disclosures created a widespread demand from the public and the press as well as the medical community to legally ban trading in organs. Thus, was born the present enactment (1995; 611).

The purpose of The Transplantation of Human Organs Act, 1994[2], according to Bandhyopadhyay and Gupta, is "to provide for the regulation of removal, storage and transplantation of human organs for therapeutic purposes and for the prevention of commercial dealings in human organs" (1997;17). According to them, "the legislation seeks to regulate organ transplantation to near relatives (parents, offspring, siblings and spouses) in the case of live donation and to remove the legal barriers to use of organs from the so called 'brain dead' people. Commercial transactions are, thus, prohibited under the purview of this Act. An authorization committee is required to be formed to monitor the transplantation programme in every state. Specific requirements are listed which hospitals must meet to get a license to perform transplantation" (Bandhyopadhyay & Gupta 1997; 17).

Commenting upon the salient features of the organ transplant legislation in India, Amalorpavanathan says that it allows doctors to certify 'brain death', thus, enabling the starting of cadaver transplantation. Within a few months of enacting this bill, he says, the first cadaveric heart transplantation took place at the All India Institute of Medical Sciences, Delhi (1995; 611).

Apart from this, the Indian enactment on transplantation also enables near relatives to donate a kidney under the assumption that near relatives are more likely to provide a kidney with matching tissue characteristics which is essential for transplantation. According to Bavinck, "The aim of matching tissue characteristic is to discover as many similarities as possible between the cell and tissue types of the donor and those of the recipient. The more closely the tissue structures of the recipient and the donor resemble one another, the less likely it is that the defense system of the recipient will identify

2. The Transplantation of Human Organs Act is elaborated in the appendix.

the donor tissue as 'foreign'. This reduces the immune response and increases the chance of success. Matching, however, means that the blood groups of the donor and the recipient must be compatible, although they do not have to be the same. The weight and dimensions of the donor organ must also match with that of the recipient, that is, within a margin of 25%" (1996; 29). As it is clear, the best kidney donor is the one whose tissue characteristics match with the recipient and this, according to Bavinck, is more likely to be obtained when the donor and the recipient are blood relatives (1996; 29).

Interestingly, the Act includes spouses among the category of near relatives. This raises a few interesting sociological questions. The wife as a donor assumes a lot of importance in the Indian social context. While in North India which practices exogamic marriage, any two persons who marry have to be unrelated by blood (that is, they do not have to be near relatives), in parts of south India, the preferred from of marriage is between cross cousins or between mother's brother and sister's daughter. Therefore, in the North Indian context, although, a spouse will not be medically suitable as a donor, yet, we find in the observations of several scholars and doctors that it is the wife who is the most common donor for men. For Doctor Vijay Kher[3], "... in cases of related donations, it is usually the wife or a poor brother who ends up sacrificing a kidney" (Vij and Kalghatgi; 1998). Similarly, Doctor Dash[4] says, "out of 10 donors in the spouse category, it is the wife in 9 cases who gifts her kidney to the husband" (Vij and Kalghatgi; 1998). Amalorpavanathan supports his statement on females (wives) donating a larger number of organs and fewer females receiving organs for transplantation with the data given by him in Table below but the data is incomplete because it does not tell us the comparative incidence of organ failure among males and females who require

3. Doctor Vijay Kher is the Head of Nephrology at the Indraprastha Apollo Hospital, New Delhi (Vij and Kalghatgi; 1998).
4. Doctor Dash is a Nephrologist at the All India Institute of Medical Sciences, New Delhi.

transplantation. Amalorpavanathan's statement that female kidney failure patients do not get transplants in the same proportion as males would be more meaningful if there are figures showing that there are equal number of male and female kidney failure patients but while males get transplants, the females do not.

Table : 4.1

Proportion of Males and Females Getting Transplants and Donating Organs for Transplantation (from July 1987 to March 1995)

	Male	*Female*	*Total*
No. of Actual Organ Donors	110	173	283
No. of Transplants Performed	223	60	283

Amalorpavanathan 1995;611

According to Amalorpavanathan, "a spouse does not seem to be a right choice in the Indian social context because in a male dominated country such as India, such a clause will put a moral pressure on the wife to donate her kidney to the husband if he needs one" (1995; 611). He argues that it is both medically and sociologically unacceptable to include spouse in the list of 'near relatives' who can donate their kidneys (1995; 611). The Act should address itself to this anomaly whereby it is the non blood related near relative, that is, the wife who is donating her kidney more often than other blood related near relatives. Amalorpavanathan goes further and argues that close relatives other than the immediately related brother, sister, father, mother, daughter, spouse, son should also be included in the list of near relatives as they share the same sort of consanguinous relationship with the patient. He argues that if these relatives are included in the list of 'near relatives', it would enlarge the number of donors available to the patient and one can choose the best matching kidney (1995; 611).

Another important flaw in the Indian transplant legislation, according to Amalorpavanathan, relates to the clause wherein an actually unrelated person could donate his kidney by reason of affection or attachment to the recipient or any other special reason. According to him, this aspect of the Act constitutes an important flaw because it is not difficult for a person to prove his affection or attachment for another and, thus, it allows for the organ trade to continue stealthily in the black markets (1995; 612).

Amalorpavanathan's view finds support in Rothman's description of how the Act is flouted in India. According to him, the requirement of the donor being attached to the recipient can be easily met. As he says, "the brokers and buyers coach the donors on what to say to the committee set up to authorize such donations that he is, for example, a cousin and that he had a photograph of a family gathering to prove it, or that he is a close friend and bears great affection for the potential recipient" (Rothman 1998; 15). According to Doctor Dash, "the touts bring a woman and say that she is the wife of the recipient. Since most people don't have marriage certificates or any other proof, there is no way of verifying the facts" (Vij and Kalghatgi; 1998). Similarly, Poornima Joshi - a journalist reports in 'Hindustan Times', Delhi, that "it is not difficult for brokers and unscrupulous doctors to tutor the concerned people. As both parties (donors and recipients) have a reason to insist that the donation is voluntary, there is no way that the authorisation committee can check whether money has exchanged hands in the process" (Hindustan Times, December 10, 2000). Rothman argues that "exposing these fictions would be simple enough, but many committees immediately approve them, unwilling to block transactions that bring large sums to hospitals, surgeons and brokers" (1998; 15). The practical scenario of the organ markets in India is, according to Amalorpavanathan, the same as prior to the enactment of the legislation : As usual, the rich Arab flies down to Bombay; The poor migrant labourer from Dháravi donates his kidney to him 'by reason of affection or attachment' (1995; 612).

Another unfortunate aspect of the Act is that not all states of the country have adopted this law[5]. Therefore, the main thrust of the act - to ban commercial dealings in organs is severely hampered because of lack of all India applicability of the transplant Act. Since such states as Punjab, Gujarat, Rajasthan and U.P. have not yet adopted this act, this has left sufficient space for those who intend to violate the provisions of the law and make money.

It is clear from the above description that the ideology intended to be propagated through the Indian legislation is undoubtedly - the 'gift' ideology. Quite similar to the American transplant Act, the Indian legislation on procurement of organs seeks to engender the morality and altruism involved in gift transactions between individuals with the sole purpose of helping a relative or a stranger in need. Ironically enough, a legislation which aims at propagating the 'gift' ideology disguises the 'market' ideology in its sub clause. Thus, the human organ transplant legislation in India has a limited scope for eliminating the unethical trading in organs. According to Doctor Dash, "the procedure laid down by the law is elaborate but that doesn't stop people from finding holes in it" (Vij and Kalghatgi; 1998). Similarly, Poornima Joshi - a journalist opines that "the banning of organ trade has only helped touts and unscrupulous medical practitioners". She argues that "the unrealistic approach of the law has resulted in exploitation of poor who sell their organs" (Hindustan Times, December 10, 2000). Doctor Mani[6], too, feels that "The law which was meant to prohibit commercial dealings in human organs now provides protection for these very

---

5. The Law applies to all the states and all the union territories of India which adopt this Act by resolution passed in that behalf under clause (1) of Article 252 of the Constitution.
6. Doctor Mani is the Chief Nephrologist at the Indraprastha Apollo Hospital in Chennai.

commercial dealings" (Hindustan Times, Delhi, December 10, 2000). Amalorpavanathan, goes to the extent of arguing that the law has legitimized the exploitation of the poor by the rich in one more way (1995; 612).

International Laws

According to Fluss (1991), the following international bodies have enacted legislations to ban the commercialization or trading of organs.

* the Thirty – Seventh World Medical Assembly convened by the World Medical Association in 1985 noted that a trade involving considerable financial gain had developed in developing countries for transplantation of live kidneys to Europe and the USA. It condemned the purchase and sale of human organs for transplantation and called on the governments of all countries to take steps to prevent the commercial use of human organs. At the Thirty-Ninth World Medical Assembly in 1987, a declaration on human organ transplantation was adopted in which the purchase and sale of human organs for transplantation was condemned (1991; 307).

* A United Arab Draft law on Human Organ Transplants, as Fluss states, was adopted by the Council of Arab Ministers of Health in 1987. Article 7 of the law lays down that the sale, purchase or remunerated donation of organs is prohibited and that no specialist, knowing an organ to have acquired by such means, may use it in a transplant operation (1991; 308).

* In 1978, the Committee of Ministers of the Council of Europe adopted a resolution on the harmonization of the legislation of member states relating to the removal, grafting and transplantation of human substances (1991; 308).

* Further, in 1987, Fluss points out that a conference of European health ministers issued a text on the non – commercialization of human organs which stated that a human organ must not be offered for profit by any organ exchange organization, organ banking centre or by any other organization or individual. It also warned against advertising for donations or transplantation by organization or individuals outside their national territory (1991; 308).

* In 1989, Fluss informs that the Fourteenth International Congress on Penal law called for the prevention of the commercialization of human organs and tissues, if necessary, by penal sanctions and for national and international measures to prevent the utilization of organs and tissues obtained through the exploitation of the economic needs of donors or their relatives (1991; 310).

Fluss informs that W.H.O. after following extensive consultations, developed a set of 'Guiding Principles on Human Organ Transplantation' in 1991 when the Forty-fourth World Health Assembly recommended the member states to formulate policies in this area. The guiding principles are intended to provide an orderly, ethical and acceptable framework for regulating the acquisition and transplantation of human organs. The term 'human organs', he clarifies, is used here to cover organs and tissues with the exception of reproductive tissues namely ova, spermatozoa, ovaries, testicles, embroys and blood and blood constituents for transfusion purposes. The guiding principles prohibit giving and receiving money as well as any other commercial dealings in this field but do not affect the payment of expenses incurred in organ recovery, presentation and supply. W.H.O's particular concern is the protection of minors and other vulnerable persons from coercion and improper inducement to donate organs (1991; 309).

According to the above mentioned guiding principles,

organs and tissues may be removed from the bodies of deceased and living persons for the purpose of transplantation only in accordance with the following principles (Fluss 1991; 309) :

* Organs may be removed from the bodies of deceased persons for the purpose of transplantation if :

    (a) Any consents required by law are obtained; and

    (b) There is no reason to believe that the deceased person objected to such removal in the absence of any formal consent given during the person's life time.

* Physicians determining that the death of a potential donor has occurred should not be directly involved in organ removal from the donor and subsequent transplantation procedures, or be responsible for the care of potential recipients of such organs.

* Organs for transplantation should be removed preferably from the bodies of deceased persons. However, adult living persons may donate organs, but in general such donors should be genetically related to the recipients. Exceptions may be made in the case of transplantation of bone marrow and other acceptable regenerative tissues.

An organ may be removed from the body of an adult living donor for the purpose of transplantation if the donor gives free consent. The donor should be free of any undue influence and pressure and sufficiently informed to be able to understand and weigh the risks, benefits and consequences of consent.

* No organ should be removed from the body of a living minor for the purpose of transplantation. Exceptions may be made under national law in the case of regenerative tissues.

* The human body and its parts cannot be the subject of commercial transactions. Accordingly, giving or receiving payment (including any other compensation or reward) for organs should be prohibited.

* Advertising the need for or availability of organs, with a view to offering or seeking payment, should be prohibited.

* It should be prohibited for physicians and other health professionals to engage in organ transplantation procedures if they have reason to believe that the organs concerned have been the subject of commercial transactions.

* It should be prohibited for any person or facility involved in organ transplantation procedures to receive any payment that exceeds a justifiable fee for the services rendered.

* In the light of the principles of distributive justice and equity, donated organs should be made available to patients on the basis of medical need and not on the basis of financial or other considerations.

The List of Member states according to WHO region which are known to have legislation against commerce in human organs.[7]

America

Argentina
Bolivia
Brazil
Canada
Chile
Columbia
Costa Rica
Cuba
Dominican Republic
Ecuador
Gautemala
Honduras
Mexico
Panama
USA
Venezuela

7. *Source:* Fluss, Sev S. 1991. "Commerce in Human Organs: The International Response". World Health Forum. Vol. 12; 308. In 1994, India also enacted a legislation against commerce in human organs.

Europe

Austria	Italy
Belgium	Luxemberg
Denmark	Romania
Finland	Spain
France	Switzerland
Germany	Turkey
Greece	United Kingdom
Hungary	Yugoslavia

Eastern Mediterranean

Cyprus	Lebanon
Iraq	Syrian Arab Republic
Kuwait	Tunisia

Africa

Algeria
Malawi
South Africa
Zimbabwe

Western Pacific

Australia
Singapore

South-East Asia

Indonesia
Sri Lanka

The Legal Provisions - A Comparative Analysis

A brief comparison of the laws of different lands described above suggests that the rights of donors, alive or cadaver, in so far as the latter can be said to have rights, as well as the rights of recipients have not been clearly spelled out. The rights of live donors does not pose a major legal problem so long as they have been properly informed about the risks involved and the uncertainty of success and who still agree to donate their organs (kidneys) in writing. However, in those cases where monetory transactions are involved, the rights of living donors and recipients are severely hampered because of the restriction put by the state on commercial transactions in organs which is actually the case in most countries. In the Indian context one encounters this problem in large measure because on the one hand the transplant Act in India permits donations of organs by live persons only to 'near relatives'. On the other hand, it permits unrelated persons to donate kidney 'by reason of affection or attachment', thus, creating considerable confusion and ambiguity regarding an individual's rights to donate his organs.

The rights of a cadaver donor, however, poses a special problem. In the first place, a lot of care, alertness and emergency planning is required so that the kidneys or other organs can be removed within the medically stipulated time period so that they can be used for transplantation. There are, thus, three legal options in this context. Either the individuals, when healthy and alive, agree to donate their organs after death. In such a case where the will of a dead person is clearly available and, therefore, executed by his relatives, the rights of an individual are more or less clear but in the event of there being no written document supporting an individual's consent to organ removal after his death, the state might authorize the next of kin to give their consent. In this case again, the rights do not seem to be clear. First of all who constitutes the 'next of kin'? This question has not been properly addressed in laws of most countries. The U.S. is particularly vague in defining this category of relatives. Sweden resurrects the 'traditional' kin ties without defining what is meant by 'tradition' and Italy recognizes the relatives to second degree in constituting the category of 'next of kin' but these are all ambiguous categories that have not been properly defined[8]. India, however, seems to be clear on this issue and defines the category of 'near' relatives.

---

8. Because of the limited availability of literature on the notion of family, kin and relatives as defined in transplant Acts in the U.S., China, Italy, Sweden and Great Britain, the discussion on this aspect is also limited.

Further, in those cases where a written authorized document from the deceased prior to his death is not available, the state might also permit the removal of organs without informing the relatives. This is the policy of China which permits the removal of organs from the bodies of executed prisoners without their own or their kins' consent. In such a case when an individual's consent to removal of his organ after death is not seen as mandatory or even required, there is, clearly, no question of an individual's right which seems to have been taken away by the Chinese state. The Chinese case lends support to Beecher's statement that "a cadaver does not have a right to his organ removal" (1969; 97).

The most important party to have been left ignored by law in this kind of a relationship of give and take of organs is the recipient. In the laws of almost all the countries described in this chapter, the rights of the recipient have not been addressed at all. There are several circumstances under which, even if the organ is available, the patient may not like to accept it on ethical grounds. For example if the spouse, son, brother, sister or any other family member, disapproves of the donation or if the recipient gets to know that the donor is handicapped, an old person, a prisoner or a lunatic, he might consider it undesirable to accept it. Similarly, a patient might not like to take an organ from a person who is under any kind of constraint to give. Such ethical considerations on the part of a recipient are clearly left unaddressed in the legal domain of transplantation.

Another issue left unnoticed in the transplant legislations is the obligation to give and receive an organ. The transplant legislation in most countries permits organ donations from individuals if they are given voluntarily by the donors. However, Beecher points out that the donor might not really be a volunteer but may be under an obligation and pressure from the family to donate (1969; 95). Beecher questions, whether it is really ever possible to exercise truly free choice in such obligatory situations occurring in families. He also points out that there are strong internal pressures on each possible donor which are often rooted in common religious and social attitudes concerning self sacrifice : The obligation and the family pressures are often so great that it is not just difficult but rather impossible to determine if the donor is truly a volunteer (1969; 95). It is generally assumed that the patient is always eager to receive a donated organ once it is available. However, as Beecher argues, the patient may sometimes be under an obligation to accept a kidney from a relative (1969; 95). This argument about the obligation to receive an organ finds echo in the Maussian idea of the obligation to give and receive gifts as found by him among the Maori people. Mauss shows (1967) that in the 'Kula' ceremonial exchange cycle, a person is under an obligation not only to give but also to receive gifts. Similarly, in the context of transplantation, the patient in a family may be under an obligation to accept an organ. In view of the above, it can be said that the law merely lays down that the organ should be given (donated) and received as a gift but ignores the obligations that underlie such a donation and acceptance. There is a need to have proper provisions to take into account and determine such obligations. It will be an interesting sociological question to identify the cultural constraints on the patients compelling them to receive the gifts of organs or restraining them from accepting them.

To determine such obligations as they arise in family situations, it is important to understand the structure and composition of family. As Chowanek and Binik (1982; 1551) argued, 'It is within the social context of the family that an illness occurs and its management is resolved". Evidently, the obligations to donate or receive an organ would differ according to the structure and composition of the family. The most significant study in this context is Turner-Musa et al.'s study on family structure and patient survival in American end stage renal disease population. They defined family structure in terms of a patient's marital status and household composition to determine the obligations to give or receive an organ within the family. They divided families into 2 categories - simple and complex. The simple family includes patients who live with their spouses only. The complex family, on the other hand, includes patients who live with their spouses and / or other relative/non relatives. The authors found that family members' obligations towards each other are greater in simple families than in complex families (1999; 1334-1335). It could, thus, be said that while in the families of the complex type, the patient's role of bread winner may be taken up by members other than the spouse, in simple families, the spouse is the only person to look up to in the situation of crisis because of greater inter-dependence between the spouses. Hence, the two studies indicate that mutual obligations are greater in simple than in complex families. It may, therefore, be argued that the prevailing structure and composition of the family in a given cultural context must be taken into consideration in order to determine such obligations as that of giving or receiving an organ if a culturally sensitive transplant policy is to be framed in a country.

Finally, it is observed that the widely proclaimed opposition to the sale of organs for transplantation from almost all major national and international medico-legal bodies challenges or rather rejects the 'market' ideology in legal framework. Evidently, it is the idealism, morality and altruism inherent in the 'gift' ideology that is sought to be promoted through such national and international legislative measures. The American and Indian transplant laws typically portray the typical Maussian altruism involved in the 'gift' ideology, relating directly the donor and the recipient. In Italy, Great Britain and Sweden (although differently), the laws promote the generalized anonymous altruism of the gift ideology indirectly mediated by the state. The Chinese legislation, however, seems to be of great relevance in this context. The Chinese legislation provides for the use of organs for transplantation from the dead bodies of executed prisoners who neither have the choice to donate voluntarily nor have the right to sell their organs. The use of the organs of executed prisoners is kept strictly confidential and as a state secret. This fact of keeping it confidential is an acknowledgement by the authorities that such a practice would be culturally and ethically inacceptable to the people in China as well as to the rest of the world. The Chinese legislation is unique in the sense that it neither completely subscribes to the 'gift' nor to the 'commodification' of organs as seen above.

It is well known that the transplantable organs are always in short supply and that societies have a powerful means of overcoming this acute shortage by resorting to the 'market' alternative. The mere rejection of 'market' ideology in legislation does not put a check on the increasing commodification and the resulting trade in organs. As Rothman points out, "despite extensive international legal and ethical provisions against commercialization of human organs, there exists a flourishing, unregulated and indeed anarchic international commerce in organs. The routes that would-be organ recipients follow are well known to both doctors and patients. Italians (who have the lowest rate of organ donations in Europe) travel to Belgium to obtain organs. So do Israelis who lately have also been going to rural Turkey and bringing their surgeon along with them. Residents of the Gulf states, Egyptians, Malaysians and Bangladeshis mainly come to India for organs. In the Pacific, Koreans, Japanese and Taiwanese along with the residents of Hong Kong and Singapore fly to China. Less frequently, south Americans go to Cuba and citizens of the former Soviet Union go to Russia. Americans for the most part stay home but well-to-do foreigners come to the United States for transplants and some centres allot upto 10% of their organs to them" (1998; 14).

Although the laws concerning what can and cannot be removed from a body and under what circumstances are variable across countries, it can be said that there is atleast one common dilemma encountered in the majority of transplant laws. This relates to making a choice between 'altruism' and 'commodification' alternatives. Should the legal policy be directed towards promoting altruism in the society or should it be directed towards increasing the supply of organs for transplantation. In addition to this dilemma, there are several other perplexing legal questions that are continuously emerging in the field of transplantation. The questions are diverse and as wide ranging as to how to determine the obligatory pressures behind an organ donor's and recipient's decision. Should 'brain death' be legalized? How to protect the human rights of the lunatics, the handicapped, the old and people in other dependent circumstances? What should be given preference — the sentiments of the deceased family or the needs of the dying patient, etc.

It is clear from the above discussion that legal problems arising in transplantation are wide ranging and will continue to be so in future. Since transplantation is a rapidly developing medical therapy, increasingly facing the challenge of providing a simple and inexpensive solution to organ failure, it will continue to pose ethical, legal and cultural questions and dilemmas. Therefore, laws will have to be continuously formulated and reformulated.

5
CONCLUSION

The detailed analysis and discussion of cross cultural perspectives on transplantation of human organs in the preceding chapters has made it possible to present some general observations.

There is little doubt that organ transplantation has been accepted worldwide as a successful medical therapy in improving and prolonging the life of organ failure patients, yet, a large number of ethico-legal and socio-cultural dilemmas are still being encountered in this area. Right from the beginning of the success of transplant surgery, its cultural dimensions have been subordinated to the medical considerations.

Sociologists and social anthropologists have underlined the importance of seeing health care systems as being closely connected with their surrounding cultural systems. Ignoring this cultural dimension, undoubtedly, constitutes a serious lapse. According to Ohnuki-Tierney, "for any medical system to cease to address ethical and cultural issues is a serious transgression of humanity" (1994; 242). This statement is very much true in the context of organ transplantation which, according to Knutson, has given rise to several moral and ethical issues of disturbing magnitude, such as the definition of human life, body, body parts, death, human rights, community welfare and the value of one as compared to other human lives. Knuston argues that an understanding of these critical issues is essential if transplant surgery is to proceed further in the prolongation of human lives (1968; 393).

It follows that the issue of organ donation and transplantation must be discussed in its socio-cultural context. Both the decisions to donate as well as to receive an organ must be seen in the realm of socio-cultural norms that guide and regulate such decisions. Following this argument, this study attempted to provide an insight into the cultural attitudes, motivations and rationale related to organ donation and transplantation. Of the several ethical questions generally raised, this study has addressed the following issues -

* Ethical issues and perspectives on organ donation.
* The organ procurement controversy between the 'gift' and the 'market' ideologies.
* A review of the transplantation legislations.

The major problem that worries transplant professionals and scholars today is the shortage of organs for transplantation. Although transplantation has revolutionized the field of medicine, there is still significant cultural ambivalence surrounding the issue of organ procurement and donation which has drastically affected the availability of organs for transplantation. This is evident in the data given by Livingston (1993; 617) for U.S. where although an estimated 25,000 potential donors are available but less than one-fifth become actual donors. According to this data, the number of transplant advised patients was 10,907 for kidneys, 5,986 for hearts, 406 for liver, 139 for heart lung, 14 for lung and 34 for pancreas. Inspite of current efforts, the number of available organs has not significantly increased and the average waiting time for a kidney has doubled from 126 days in 1987 to 237 days in 1988.

Similarly, in the United Kingdom, according to Gabr (1998; 120), 70% of the population were found to be in favour of donating their organs after death but only 25% carried donor cards. In Saudi Arabia, these figures were 88% and 14% respectively. Gabr attributes this reluctance to donate organs to values, norms and beliefs rooted in the culture. It is this cultural dimension and perspective on transplantation of human organs that has been the focus of this study.

Although organs for transplantation can be procured from both living as well as dead donors, the major source of organs are cadavers. This could be attributed to two reasons. First, the majority of transplantable organs, except kidneys and liver, cannot be offered by living beings. Secondly, the giving of organs through surgical operation involves pain, inconvenience, physical discomfort and some risk to the donor. On the other hand, there are no physical and medical problems in utilizing the cadaveric organs. However, as we have seen earlier, even cadaveric organ donation is deeply influenced by cultural considerations. This fact is not recognized by the medical fraternity.

Rothman states that "despite the widespread capacity of cadaveric organ supply recognized by the medical community to satisfy the growing demand of organs for transplantation, it is observed that there are strong cultural and religious taboos that discourage cadaver organ donations not only in countries with strong religious establishments but even in more secular ones as well" (1998; 14).

Earlier we have seen in chapter 2 that there are many culture driven reservations about cadaveric organ donations in Islamic law (according to Daar in Ohnuki-Tierney 1994), in Japan (according to Livingston 1993), in Germany (according to Hogle 1996) and in China (according to Ikels 1997). The role of culture in cadaveric organ donation is not well appreciated by the medical community.

On their part, the medical scientists are engrossed in defining death in a way which would increase the availability of organs. Consequently, the criterion of 'brain death' for declaring clinical death has been evolved. According to the concept of 'brain death', as defined by Gabr, "a person is said to have clinically died when he or she has suffered an irreversible loss of the capacity to be conscious owing to the non-functioning of the central trunk of the brain... This definition makes it possible to retrieve organs for transplantation from brainstem dead persons whose cardio respiratory systems are artificially maintained by means of technical devices" (1998; 121).

However, there is ample proof that a medical redefinition of death based on the separation between brain and cardio respiratory functioning is still the subject of significant cultural ambivalence. In certain religious and cultural traditions such as that of Jews, as Gabr shows, this concept of 'brain death' is not accepted and the older definition of death as cessation of pulse and spontaneous respiration is retained (1998;121). Such arguments, Gabr feels, can have a strong influence on public opinion which discourages the retrieval of organs from cadavers (1998;121). He gives the example of the, Muslim religious clergy which accepted the concept of 'brain death' at conferences in Kuwait in 1985 and Amman, Jordan in 1986 but this was later disputed by some political groups, thus, making the entire issue ambivalent (Gabr 1998; 121).

On the basis of his research on minority communities' attitude towards organ donation in the United States, Callender (1987; 1551) argues, "there is widespread suspicion that 'brain death' might be declared prematurely to provide access to organs for transplantation". According to him, the intensive care nurses find it difficult to explain it to the relatives why the apparently sleeping patient, with normal colour and beating heart, is actually dead (Callender 1987;1551). Callender reports substantial philosophical debate even among medical scientists on the concept of 'brain death' (1987; 1551).

As we saw earlier, Japan provides the most significant illustration of how 'brain death' is interpreted and rejected on the basis of pre-existing cultural frameworks. Ohnuki - Tierney reports substantial opposition to a definition of death based on brain activity and to a purely bio medical understanding of body organs (Ohnuki-Tierney, 1994). According to her, the Japanese are skeptical whether 'brain death' can be determined with certainty. They insist that each single condition used to define 'brain death' is necessary but the sum of these conditions does not mean that the brain has stopped functioning permanently. For them, the inactive brain represents a prolongation of life rather than a prolongation of the process of dying because a human body is considered 'more than an appendage of the brain' (1994; 234).

There is no doubt that the recognition and acceptance of declaring a person dead by the cessation of brain activity is an important prerequisite for the success of transplantation therapy but, unfortunately, there are substantial ethico-cultural objections to it which need to be overcome

Culture is not always antithetical to the idea of organ donation. As we saw earlier, the cultural metaphors of 'gift' and 'market' can be invoked to encourage people to donate organs. However, as we saw earlier, there is a dilemma involved in making a choice between these two. As we saw in chapter 3, at one extreme are the proponents of the 'gift' ideology who seek to evoke altruistic ideas and emotions such as generosity, selflessness and cultural heroism among donors of organs. Such altruistic values, according to Joralemon, get sanctioned by the religious authorities who pronounce organ donation as 'giving the gift of life' (1995; 343). At the other extreme are the proponents of the 'market' ideology who feel that the 'gift' ideology cannot provide sufficient number of organs. On their part, they consider it immoral to waste human organs when they are so much in demand and have the potential to save so many human lives.

The 'market' ideologues, according to Joralemon, argue

that "the rising shortage of donors would eventually force the application of market principles of demand and supply to organ procurement" (1995; 344). Moreover, when all those involved in transplantation including doctors, hospitals and other medical staff can earn profit from it, then why deny some monetary benefit to the donor of the organ. Joralemon, thus, provides a justification for granting full property rights (including sale) to an individual over his body (1995; 340). The market approach, as we saw earlier, is criticized as being unethical and exploitative leading to the commodification of body parts which give rise to violations of human rights.

Thus, both the 'gift' as well as 'market' procurement strategies are insufficient in themselves to fulfil the required need of organs for transplantation. Nevertheless, according to Joralemon, both the proposals have gained enough acceptance to be the subject of debate rather than of dismissal (1995; 346). For him, both the cultural metaphors, namely, 'gift giving' and 'property rights', have been invoked as ideological supports for encouraging organ donation. The idea is to make use of the culturally familiar concepts to legitimize organ donation (Joralemon 1995; 342-343).

The ultimate solution to the acute problem of organ shortage seems to be a middle ground that would combine the fruits of 'market' and 'gift' ideologies. Perry emphasizes that such a middle path should be so designed as not to violate moral principles of the society (1981; 163).

The controversy between the 'gift' and 'market' ideologies gets further institutionalized in the legal domain. The legal sphere is a crucial area in every society where organ access and procurement issues are codified and structured keeping into consideration the distinct cultural concepts and beliefs concerning bodies and body parts.

A brief review of transplant related legislations across nations reveals a tendency to reject commodification of organs and adopt an organ donation policy consistent with the 'gift' or altruistic ideology. The review also showed that the Chinese legislation is neither consistent with the 'gift' nor with the 'market' ideology but is highly critical of the commodification of body parts.

The Indian legal enactment on transplantation called 'The Transplantation of Human Organs Act, 1994' seeks to curb the trade in organs by permitting only the near relatives to donate organs under the assumption that money will not be exchanged between near relatives. The Act also permits donations by reason of affection or attachment to the patient. In doing so, this legislation promotes the altruism of the 'gift'.

Thus, it is observed that the widely acclaimed opposition to the sale and purchase of organs for transplantation from almost all major national and international medico-legal bodies challenges or rather rejects the 'market' ideology in the legal framework. Clearly, it is the morality and altruism of the 'gift' ideology that is sought to be promoted through various national and international legislative measures.

It must, however, be pointed out that mere rejection of 'market' ideology in legislation does not put a check on the increasing commodification and resulting trade in organs. Despite extensive legal and ethical provisions against commercialization of human organs, there exists a flourishing international trade in organs.

It is evident that the common dilemma encountered in the majority of transplant laws is to make a choice between 'altruism' and 'commodification' alternatives. Should the legal policy be directed towards promoting altruism in the society? Should it be directed towards increasing the supply of organs for transplantation? The dilemma is still unresolved and will continue to be so unless these issues are more seriously addressed. There is a need to check and penalize the trading of organs with greater strictness. Probably such stringent efforts as Rothman (1998; 17) suggests, such as establishing a permanent monitoring body and keeping a close surveillance on organ donation practices would be helpful in checking the illegal trade in organs. Such measures are more likely to have an impact if they are seriously pursued by the state, media and the public.

To conclude, the dilemma between the 'gift' and 'market' alternatives seems to be never ending both in the cultural as well as legal domains. Both sides have strong convincing arguments in their own favour. No one alternative can be totally ignored or discarded. There is, therefore, a need to evolve a multipronged approach towards procurement of organs that includes the views of legal experts, politicians, human rights organizations, social scientists as well as medical practitioners.

Organs from animals : the ultimate solution?

The critical shortage of human organs together with their growing demand and rapid technological advancement has brought about radical significant improvements in the efficacy of transplantation as a medical threapy. Doctor Praveen Sareen[1] says, "The advent of new immunosuppressive agents and confidence in the surgical techniques emboldened us to offer a third transplant to a patient with end stage renal disease" (Transplant Trends 2000;4). Williams points out that body organs are not only interchangeable at the human to human level but also at the interspecies level, that is, from animals to humans. The interspecies transplant is also known as xenotransplantation (1997;1043).

The use of animal organs for transplantation into human beings offers a new hope of meeting the current shortage of human organs for transplantation. According to Bavinck, "the advantage

1. Doctor Praveen Sareen is a leading, senior consultant transplant surgeon at R.K. Hospital, Amritsar, India.

of using animal organs is the fact that the patient does not have to wait a long time for a donor organ to become available. Animals can be bred for the purpose, thus, creating a limitless supply of donor organs" (1996; 84). It may also be argued that xenotransplantation would eliminate the moral and ethical dilemmas encountered in the removal of organs from living or cadaver human donors. However, not everyone would agree with this view.

According to Veatch, "if the mixing of genetic material from two humans raises ethical and cultural problems, then, it is but natural to expect the possibility of interspecies transplantation to be even more ethically charged" (1989; 202). According to Daar, "Xenotransplantation transgresses those boundaries which define us as human and so challenge and threaten our identity and sense of order" (1999; 54). Others may find the mixing of genetic material from the different species as violation of the natural processes ordained by God. As Veatch puts it, "Are we violating God's plan for creation when we mix genetic material from two different species?" (1989; 202).

According to Williams, "xenotransplantation raises thorny questions about the meaning of self identity. If an animal, for example, pig, is seen as a ritually unclean, then, how do we see ourselves with an animal heart inside us? Does the body become degraded, defiled or debased in some w y as a consequence and if so, what implications does this 'grotesque' body have for our sense of who and what we are?" (1997; 1044).

Although, it may appear that only organs from animals can overcome the problem of organ shortage for transplantation, Obermann argues that "once a clinical xenografting is implemented, it is highly likely that a vigorous debate on the ethics of such an intervention will take place" (1997; 311).

BIBLIOGRAPHY

Adams, Richard N. 1955. "A Nutritional Research Program in Gautemala", in B.D. Paul (ed.), *Health Culture and Community*. New York : Russell Sage Foundation.

Amalorpavanathan, J. 1995. "Transplantation of Human Organs Bill : Curate's Egg", *Economic and Political Weekly*. March 25 : 611-612.

Amundsen, D.W. 1996. *Medicine Society and Faith in the Ancient and Medieval World.* Baltimore : John Hopkins University Press.

Andrews, Lori. 1986. *My Body, My Property.* Hastings Center Report.

Angrosino, Michael V. 1994. "Comments", *Current Anthropology*. Volume 35. No. 3 : 242-243.

Bandhyopadhyay, Siddhartha and Sudip Gupta. 1997. *The Transplantation of Human Organs Act, 1994 : A Critique.* New Delhi : Allied Publishers Ltd.

Bavinck, Willem. 1996. *84 questions on Organ Transplantation.* The Netherlands : De Tijdstroom, Utrecht.

Beecher, Henry K. 1969. "Scarce Resources and Medical Advancement", in Paul A Freund (ed.), *Experimentation With Human Subjects.* United States of America : George Braziller, Inc.

Belk, Russell W. 1990. "Me and Thee Versus Mine and Thine: How Perceptions of the Body Influence Organ Donation and Transplantation", in J. Shanteau and R. Harris (eds.), *Organ Donation and Transplantation.* Washington D.C.: American Psychological Association.

Bellah, Robert N. 1973. *Emile Durkheim : On Morality and Society.* Chicago : Chicago University Press.

Benoist, Jean and Pascal Cathebras. 1993. "The Body from an Immateriality to Another". *Social Science and Medicine.* Volume 36. No. 7 : 857-865.

Berry, Phil. M. 1999. "Organ Donation : Can the U.S. Do Better?", *British Medical Journal.* Volume 319 : 1445.

Black, Peter M. and Michael T. Zervas. 1994. "Declaration of Brain Death in Neurosurgical and Neurological Practice", *Neurosurgery.* Volume 15 : 170-171.

Blumstein, James F. 1993. "The Use of Financial Incentives in Medical Care. The Case of Commerce in Transplantable Organs", *Health Matrix.* Volume 3 : 1-30.

Brams, Marvin. 1977. "Transplantable Human Organs : Should Their Use Be Authorized by State Statute?", *American Journal of Law and Medicine.* Volume 3 : 183-195.

Brim, Orville G., Howard E. Freeman., Sol Levine and Norman A. Scotch (eds.). 1970. *The Dying Patient.* New York: Russell Sage Foundation.

Byrne, Paul. A. and Richard G. Nilges. 1993. "The Brain Stem in Brain Death : A Critical Review", *Issues in Law and Medicine.* Volume 9 : 3-21.

Callender C.O., J.A. Bayton., C Yeager and J.E. Clark. 1982. "Attitudes Among Blacks Toward Donating Kidneys for Transplantation", *Journal of the National Medical Association.* Volume 74. No. 8 : 807-809.

Calne, R.Y. 1971. *Clinical Organ Transplantation.* Cambridge: Blackwell Scientific Publication.

Carrier, James G. 1995. *Gifts and Commodities* : Exchange and Western Capitalism Since 1700. London : Routledge.

Chakravarti, A.K. and S. Shamim Ahmad. 1983. "Some Socio-Geographic Aspects of Renal Transplant Cases in Saskatchewan", *Social Science & Medicine.* Volume 17. No. 12 : 829-835.

Chapman, David E. 1983. "Retailing Human Organs Under the Uniform Commercial Code", *John Marshall Law review.* Volume 16 : 393-417.

Charmaz, Kathy. 1980. *The Social Reality of Death.* California: Addison Wesley Publishing Company.

Cheal, David. 1988. *The Gift Economy.* London : Routledge.

Chengappa, Raj. 1990. "The Organs Bazaar", *India Today* : 30-37.

Chiba, Tokuji. 1981. *Essays on Seppuku*. Tokyo : Kodansha.

Chowanec, Gregory D. and Y. M. Binik. 1982. "End Stage Renal Disease (ESRD) and the Marital Dyad", *Social Science and Medicine.* Volume 16 : 1551-1558.

Christiansen, Cindy L., Steven L. Gortmaker., Jean M. Williams., Carol L. Beasley., Lori E. Brigham., Carie Capossela., Mary E. Matthiesen and Susan Gunderson. 1998. "A Method for Estimating Solid Organ Donor Potential by Organ Procurement Region", *American Journal of Public Health.* Volume 88. No. 11 : 1645-1650.

Clark, David. 1993. *The Sociology of Death. Cambridge* : Blackwell Publishers.

Cohen, Lloyd. 1989. "Increasing the Supply of Transplant Organs: The Virtue of a Futures Market", *George Washington Law Review*. Volume 58 : 1-51.

Creecy, Robert F. and Roosevelt Wright. 1990. "Correlates of Willingness to Consider Organ Donation Among Blacks",

Social Science and Medicine. Volume 31 : 1229-1232.

Curran, William J. 1969. "Governmental Regulation of the Use of Human Subjects in Medical Research : The Approach of Two Federal Agencies", in Paul. A. Freund (ed.), *Experimentation with Human Subjects.* United States of America : George Braziller.

Daar, A.S. 1989. "Ethical Issues : A Middle East Perspective", *Transplantation Proceedings.* Volume 21 : 1402-1404.

_______, 1992. "Rewarded Gifting", *Transplantation Proceedings*. Volume 24 : 2207-2211.

_____, 1999. "Animal to Human Organ Transplants - A Solution or A New Problem?", *Bulletin of the World Health Organization*. Volume 77 (1) : 54-61.

Daar, A.S. and P. Marshall. 1998. "Culture and Psychology in Organ Transplantation", *World Health Forum*. Volume 19 : 124-132.

Davis, Ronald M. 1999. "Meeting the Demand for Donor Organs in the U.S.", *British Medical Journal*. Volume 319 : 1382-1383.

Dechesser. A.D. 1986. "Organ Donation : The Supply / Demand Discrepancy", *Heart and Lung*. Volume 15 : 547-551.

Deutsches, Arzteblatt. 1993. *In Service of the Public.* Volume 90 (49) : B-2422-2423.

Dorson, Mary J. 1997. *Contours of Death and Disease in Modern England*. New York : Cambridge University Press.

Douglas, Mary. 1982. *Natural Symbols. Explorations in Cosmology.* New York : Pantheon Books.

Dukeminier, Jesse Jr. 1970. *"Supplying Organs for Transplantation" Michigan Law Review.* Volume 68 : 811-866.

Durkheim, Emile. 1984. *Division of Labour in Society*. London: Macmillan.

Economist. 1994. Volume. 333. No. 7882. (September 3).

Edsalli, Geoffrey. 1969. "The Ethical Design of Human Experiments", in Paul. A. Freund (ed.), *Experimentation with Human Subjects.* United States of America : George Braziller, Inc.

Eurotransplant Foundation Annual Report. 1993.

__________, 1994.

Exley, Catherine., Julius Sim., Norma Reid., Simon Jackson and Nick West. 1996. "Attitudes and Beliefs Within the Sikh Community Regarding Organ Donation : A Pilot Study", *Social Science and Medicine*. Volume 43. No. 1 : 23 28.

Fact Sheet For U.S. Transplant Games. 1994.

Fano, Alix. 1997. *Lethal Laws : Animal Testing, Human Health and Environmental Policy.* London : Zed Books Ltd.

Feldman, Eric. A. 1988. "Defining Death : Organ Transplants, Tradition and Technology in Japan", *Social Science and Medicine*. Volume 27. No. 4 :339-343.

Field, David R. 1988. "Maternal Brain Death during Pregnancy : Medical and Ethical Issues", *Journal of the American Medical Association* : 260-816.

Fluss, Sev. S. 1991. "Commerce in Human Organs : The International Response", *World Health Forum*. Volume 12: 307-310.

Foster, George M. and Barbara Gallentin Anderson. 1978. *Medical Anthropology*. U.S.A : John Wiley & Sons.

Fox, Renee C. and Judith P. Swazey. 1992. Spare Parts : *Organ Replacement in American Society.* Oxford : Oxford University Press.

Fox, Renee C. and Judith P. Swazey. 1974. The Courage to Fail: *A Social View of Organ Transplants and Dialysis*. Chicago : University of Chicago Press.

Fracs, Allen and D.M. Richard. 1990. *A Manual of Renal Transplantation.* London : Edward Arnold.

Freund, Paul. A. (ed.). 1969. *Experimentation with Human Subjects.* New York : George Braziller, Inc.

Frontier. December. 1997.

Frontline. December 1997.

Gaber, A.O., G. Hall., D.C. Phillips., E.A. Tolly and L.G. Britt. 1990. "Survey of Attitudes of Health Care Professionals Towards Organ Donation", *Transplantation roceedings.* Volume 22 : 313-315.

Gabr, Mamdouh. 1996. "Organ Transplantation in Developing Countries", *World Health Forum.* Volume 19 : 120-23.

Gerhardt, Uta 1990. "Patient Careers in End-Stage Renal Failure", *Social Science and Medicine.* Volume 30. No. 11 : 1211-1224.

Giacomini, Mita. 1997. "A Change of Heart and a Change of Mind? Technology and the Redefinition of Death in 1968", *Social Science and Medicine.* Volume 44. No. 10 : 1465-1482.

Giddens, Anthony. 1972. *Emile Durkheim : Selected Writings*. London : Cambridge University Press.

Godelier, Maurice. 1996. *The Enigma of the Gift.* France : Polity Press.

Gordon I., R. Turner and T.W. Price. 1963. *Medical Jurisprudence.* Great Britain : E & S. Livingstone Ltd.

Graburn, Nelson N.H. and B. Stephan Strong. 1973. *Circumpolar Peoples : An Anthropological Perspective.* Pacific Palisades : Goodyear.

Gregory, Weiss and Lynne Lonnquist. 1996. *The Sociology of Health, Healing and Illness.* United States of America : A&A Publishing Services.

Gutkind, Lee. 1988. Many Sleepless Nights : *The World of Organ Transplantation.* New York : W.W. Norton.

Haraway, Donna Jeanne. 1989. *Primate Visions : Gender, Race and Nature in the World of Modern Science.* New York: Routledge.

Harris, Lisa E., Friedrich C. Luft., David W. Rudy and William M. Tierney. 1995. "Correlates of Health Care Satisfaction in Inner-city Patients With Hypertension and Chronic Renal Insufficiency", *Social Science and Medicine.* Volume41. No. 12 : 1639-1645.

Havighurst, Clark C. 1967. *Medical Progress and the Law.* United States of America : Duke University.

Hazony, Orly. 1993. "Increasing the Supply of Cadaver Organs for Transplantation : Recognizing that the Real Problem is Psychological not Legal", *Health Matrix.* Volume 3 : 219-257.

Hertz, Robert. 1960. *Death and the Right Hand.* Glencoe : Free Press.

Hogle, Linda F. 1996. "Transforming Body Parts into Therapeutic Tools : A Report from Germany", *Medical Anthropology Quarterly* 10 (4) : 675-682.

Holder, Angela Roddey. 1978. *Medical Malpractice Law.* Canada: John Wiley & Sons.

Horton, Raymond L. and Patricia J. Horton. 1990. "Knowledge Regarding Organ Donation : Identifying and Overcoming Barriers to Organ Donation", *Social Science and Medicine.* Volume 31. No. 7 : 791-800.

Hosaka, Yasamasu. 1992. *Organ Transplantation and the*

Japanese. Tokyo : Asahi Sonorama.

Human Rights Watch Commission Special Report. 1993. January 12.

Hume, David M. 1967. "Renal Homotransplantation in Man", *Annual Review of Medicine*. Volume 18 : 229-268.

Ikels, Charlotte. 1997. "Kidney Failure and Transplantation in China", *Social Science and Medicine*. Volume 44. No.9: 1271-1283.

Inwald, David., Immanual Jakobivits and Andy Petros. 2001. "Brain Stem Death : Managing Care When Accepted Medical Guidelines and Religious Beliefs are in Conflict", *British Medical Journal*. Volume 320 : 1266-1268.

Jaffee, Erik S. 1990. "She's Got Bettee Davis('s) Eyes : Assessing the Non-Consensual Removal of Cadaver Organs Under the Takings and Due Process Clauses", *Columbia Law Review*. Volume 90 : 528-571.

Jaffee, Louis. L. 1969. "Law as a System of Control", in Paul. A. Freund (ed.), *Experimentation With Human Subjects*. U.S.A.: Braziller, Inc.

Joralemon, Donald. 1995. "Organ Wars : The Battle for Body Parts", *Medical Anthropology Quarterly*. Volume 9. No. 3 : 335-356.

Karlberg, Ingvar and Tore Schersten. 1989. "Human Organ Transplantation", *World Health Forum*. Volume 10 :228 234.

Keithmant, A. (ed.). 1965. *Taylor's Principles and Practice of Medical Jurisprudence*. United States of America : J&A. Churchill Ltd.

Kimbrell Andrew. 1993. The Human Body Sheep: *The Engineering and Marketing of Life*. San Francisco : Harper.

Knutson, Andie L. 1968. "Body Transplants and Ethical Values" *Social Science and Medicine.* Volume 2 : 393-414

Koing, Barbara A. and Linda F. Hogle. 1995. "Organ Transplantation (Re) Examined?", *Medical Anthropology Quarterly.* Volume (9) 3 : 393-397.

Lightman, Ernie S. 1982. "Technique Bias in Measuring Acts of Altruism", *Social Science and Medicine.* Volume 16 : 1627-1633.

Livingston, Ivor Lensworth. 1993. "Renal Disease and Black Americans : Selected Issues", *Social Science and Medicine.* Volume 37. No. 5 : 613-621.

Lock, Margaret. 1995. "Transcending Mortality: Organ Transplants and The Practicc of Contradictions", *Medical Anthropology Quarterly.* Volume 9 (3) : 390-399.

Low, Setha M. 1994. "Protest of the Body", *Medical Anthropology Quarterly.* Volume 8 (4) : 476-478.

Machado, Nora. 1996. "The Swedish Transplant Acts: Sociological Considerations on Bodies and Giving", *Social Science and Medicine.* Volume 42. No. 2 : 159 168.

Manners, Joh MC. 1981. *Death and the Enlightement: Changing Attitudes to Death Among Christians and Unbelievers in Enlightened Century France.* Oxford : Calender Press.

Matas, Arthur J., J. Arras., J. Muyskens., V. Tellis. and F.J. Veith. 1985. "A Proposal for Cadaver Organ Procurement : Routine Removal with Right of Informed Refusal", *Journal of Health Politics, Policy and Law.* Volume 10 : 231-244.

Mauss, Marcel. 1967. *The Gift : Forms and Functions in*

Archaic Societies. New York : W.W. Norton

Mc Dermott, Walsh. 1969. "Comment on Law as a System of Control", in Paul. A. Freund (ed.), *Experimentation with Human Subjects.* New York : George Braziller.

Mc Gough, E.A. and M.W. Chopek. 1990. "The Physician's Role as Asker in Obtaining Organ Donation", *Transplantation Proceedings.* Volume 22 : 267-272.

Medawar, P.B. 1946. *Old Age and Natural Death.* London: Methwen.

Merleau - Ponty, Maurice. 1968. *The Visible and The Invisible.* Alphonso Lingus : Northwestern University Press.

Metcalf, Peter and Richard Huntington. 1991. *Celebrations of Death: The Anthropology of Mortuary Ritual.* Cambridge: Cambridge University Press.

Miller, Henry. 1973. *Medicine and Society.* London : Oxford University Press.

Miller, W. Watts. 1996. *Durkheim, Morals and Modernity.* London : UCL Press.

Morsy, Soheir A. 1993. *Gender, Sickness and Healing in Rural Egypt : Ethnography in Historical Context.* Boulder : Westview Press

Nath, Vijay. 1987. *Dana : Gift System in Ancient India.* Delhi: Munshiram Publishers.

National Centre for Health Statistics in U.S. 1966.

National Kidney Foundation Fact Sheet 1994, U.S.

Newsweek, 1967. December 18.

Norris, M.K.G. 1990. "Required Request : Why It Has Not Significantly Improved The Donor Shortage", *Heart and Lung.* Volume 19 : 685-686.

Obermann, Konrad. 1997. "Some Politico-Economic Aspects

of Organ Shortage in Transplantation Medicine", *Social Science and Medicine.* Volume 46. No. 3 :299-311.

Ohnuki-Tierney, Emiko. 1981. *Illness and Healing Among the Sakhalin Ainu : A Symbolic Interpretation.* Cambridge: Cambridge University Press.

__________. 1984. *Illness and Culture in Contemporary Japan : An Anthropological View. Cambridge:* Cambridge University Press.

Ohnuki-Tierney, Emiko. 1994. "Brain Death and Organ Transplantation", *Current Anthropology.* Volume 35. No. 3 : 233-242.

Parkes, Colin Murray., Pittum Laungeri and Bill Young. 1997. *Death and Bereavement Across Cultures.* London : Routledge.

Parkin, Robert. 1996. *Darkside of Humanity : The Work of Robert Hertz and its Legacy.* Amsterdam : Harwood Publishers.

Perry, Clifton. 1981. "The Right of Public Access to Cadaver Organs", *Social Science and Medicine.* Volume 15F :163-166.

Peters, Thomas. 1991. "Life or Death : The Issue of Payment in Cadaveric Organ Donation", *Journal of the American Medical Association.* Volume 265. No. 10 : 1302-1305.

Plough, Alonzo L. 1981. "Medical Technology and the Crisis of Experience : The Costs of Clinical Legitimation", *Social Science and Medicine.* Volume 15F : 89-101.

Poe, E. A. 1844. "The Premature Burial", in A.H. Quinn and E.H.O' Neill (eds.), *The Complete Poems and Stories of Edgar Allan Poe.* New York : Alfred A. Knopf.

Prottas, Jeffrey M. 1983. "Encouraging Altruism : Public Attitudes and the Marketing of Organ Donation", *Milbank*

Memorial Fund Quarterly. Volume 61 : 278-306.

Prottas, Jeffrey M. 1989. "The Organization of Organ Procurement", *Journal of Health, Politics, Policy and Law.* Volume 14: 41-55.

Rabinow, Paul. 1992. "Severing the Ties: Fragmentation and Dignity in Late Modernity, Knowledge and Society", *The Anthropology of Science and Technology.* Volume 9: 168-187.

Radin, Margaret J. 1987. "Market Inalienability", *Harvard Law Review.* Volume 100 : 1849-1937.

Rana, D.S. 1996. "The Kidneys", *Hindustan Times.* March 20 : 16.

______. 1998. "Kidney Transplantation : Ground Realities", *Transplant Trends*: 4a : 4b.

Rothman, David. 1998. "The International Traffic in Human Organs", *The New York Review*. Volume XLV. No. 5: 14-17.

Rutsein, David D. 1969. "The Ethical Design of Human Experiments", in Paul. A Freund (ed.), *Experimentation with Human Subjects*. U.S.A. : Braziller.

Schubert, Hartwig Von. 1994. "Donated Blood-Gift or Commodity", *Social Science and Medicine.* Volume 39. No. 2: 201-206.

Schwindt, Richard and A. Vining. 1986. "Proposal for a Future Delivery Market for Transplant Organs", *Journal of Health Politics, Policy and Law.* Volume 11 : 483-500.

Scott, Russell. 1981. *The Body as Property*. New York : Viking Press.

Scribner, B.H., E.B. Fergus., S.T. Boen and E.D. Thomas. 1965. "Some Therapeutic Approaches to Chronic Renal Insufficiency", *Annual Review of Medicine.* Volume 16: 285-300.

Sharp, Lesley A. 1995. "Organ Transplantation as a Transformative Experience", *Medical Anthropology Quarterly.* Volume 9. No. 3: 357-389.

Silverstein, Arthur M. 1989. *History of Immunology.* London: Academic Press.

Skumanich, Stephanie A. and David P. Kintsfather. 1996. "Promoting the Organ Donor Card : A Causal Model of Persuasion Effects", *Social Science and Medicine.* Volume 43. No. 3 : 401-408.

Smith, William B. 1987. "Judeo-Christian Teaching on Euthansia", *Linacre Quarterly.* February : 27-32.

Sonada, Kyoichi. 1988. *Health and Illness in Changing Japanese Society*. Japan : University of Tokyo Press.

Sque, Magi and Sheila A. Payne. 1996. "Dissonant Loss : The Experiences of Donor Relatives", *Social Science and Medicine.* Volume 43. No. 9 : 1359-1370.

Sque, Magi., Sheila A. Payne, and Ioannis Vlachonikolis. 2000. "Cadaveric Donotransplantation : Nurses Attitudes, Knowledge and Behaviour", *Social Science and Medicine.* Volume 50 : 541-552.

Stickel, Delford L. 1967. "Organ Transplantation in Medical and Legal perspectives", in Clark C. Havighurst (ed.), *Medical Progress and The Law*. United States of America : Duke University.

Switzer, Galen E., Mary Amanda Dew., Victoria A. Butterworth., Roberta G. Simmons and Mindy Schimmel. 1997. "Understanding Donors' Motivations : A Study of Unrelated Bone Marrow Donors", *Social Science and Medicine.* Volume 45. No. 1 : 137-147.

Synnott, Anthony. 1993. *The Body Social : Symbolism, Self And Society.* New York: Routledge.

Taylor, Steve and Clive Ashworth. 1987. "Durkheim and Social Realism : An Approach to Health and Illness", in Graham Scambler (ed.), *Sociological Theory and Medical Sociology.* London and New York : Tavistock Publications.

Hindustan Times. New Delhi. December 10, 2000.

The Lancet. Volume 355. Number 9206.

The Times of India. New Delhi. August 13, 2000.

________. December 7, 2000.

________. June 28, 1998.

Titmuss, Richard. 1970. *The Gift Relationship : From Human Blood to Social Policy.* New York : Vintage.

Toynbee, Arnold and Arther Koestler. 1976. *Life After Death.* London: Weidenfeld and Nicolsen.

Transplantation of Human Organs Act, 1994. Second Edition. 1995. Lucknow : Eastern Books Company.

Transplant Trends. 2000. Volume 15.

____. 2001. Volume 17.

Trisolini, M., D. Ashley., V. Harik and W. Bicknell. 1999. "Policy Analysis for End Stage, Renal Disease in Jamaica", *Social Science and Medicine.* Volume 49 : 905-920.

Turner-Musa, Jocelyn., David Leidner., Samuel Simmens., David Reiss., Paul L. Kimmel and Barbara Holder, 1999. "Family Structure and Patient Survival in an African-American End Stage Rend Disease Population. A Preliminary Investigation", *Social Science and Medicine.* Volume 48 : 1333-1340.

United Network for Organ Sharing (UNOS) Scientific Registry. July 5. 1997.

Van Gannep, Arnold. 1961. *The Rites of Passage..* Chicago :

University of Chicago Press.

Varekamp, I., L.J. Krol and J.A.C. Danse 1998. "Age Rationing for Renal Transplantation? The Role of Age in Decisions Regarding Scarce Life Extending Medical Resources", *Social Science and Medicine.* Volume 47. No. 1 : 113 120. Veatch, Robert M. 1989. Death, Dying and the Biological Revolution: *Our Last Quest for Responsibility.* USA:Tale University Press.

Vij, Bhavna and Manjiri Kalghatgi. 1998. "The Kidney Bazaar", *The Express Magazine.* June 28 : Section 2.

Wada, Juro and Kazuo Miwa. 1992. "Cowardice Called Democracy", *Shokun.* Volume 24. No. 6 : 62-73.

Waltz, Jon R. and Fred E., Inbau. 1971. *Medical Jurisprudence.* USA: The Macmillan Company.

Williams, Simon J. 1997. "Modern Medicine and the "Uncertain Body" : From Corporeality to Hyper Reality?", *Social Science and Medicine.* Volume 45. No. 7 : 1041-1049.

Wolstenholme, Gordon, and Maeve O' Connor (eds.). 1966. *Law and Ethics of Transplantation.* London. : J&E. Churchill Ltd.

World Transplant Games Federation Report. 1998.

Yan, Yunxiang. 1996. *The Flow of Gifts : Reciprocity and Social Networks in a Chinese Village.* California : Stanford University.

Zhang, Z. 1996. "Organ Transplantation Must be Voluntary, Open and Transparent", *Medicine and Philosophy.* Volume 17. No. 3: 178-179.

Zhu, M. and Y. Liu. 1988. "Smash the Bonds of Traditional Ethics to Develop Autopsy Cause", *Medicine and philosophy.* Volume 9. No. 8 : 38-40.

APPENDIX

The Transplantation of Human Organs Act, 1994[1]
[ACT NO. 42 OF 1994]
[8th July, 1994]

An Act to provide for the regulation of removal, storage and transplantation of human organs for therapeutic purposes and for the prevention of commercial dealings in human organs and for matters connected therewith or incidental thereto.

Where it is expedient to provide for the regulation of removal, storage and transplantation of human organs for therapeutic purposes and for the prevention of commercial dealings in human organs;

And whereas Parliament has no power to make laws for the States with respect to any of the matters aforesaid except as provided in Articles 249 and 250 of the Constitution;

And whereas in pursuance oi clause (1) of Article 252 of the Constitution, resolutions have been passed by all the Houses of the Legislatures of the States of Goa, Himachal Pradesh and Maharashtra to the effect that the matters aforesaid should be regulated in those States by Parliament by law;

Be in enacted by Parliament in the Forty-fifth Year of the Republic of India as follows :-

1. Received the assent of President on July 8. 1994 and published inthe Gazette of India, Extra., Part II, Section 1, dated 11th July, 1994, pp. 1-13, No. 58.

I

PRELIMINARY

1. Short title, application and commencement.

(1) This Act may be called the Transplantation of Human Organs Act, 1994.

(2) It applies, in the first instance, to the whole of the States of Goa, Himachal Pradesh and Maharashtra and to all the Union territories and it shall also apply to such other State which adopts this Act by resolution passed in that behalf under clause (1) of Article 252 of the Constitution.

(3) It Shall come into force in the States of Goa, Himachal Pradesh and Maharashtra and in all the Union territories on such date as the Central Government may, by notification, appoint and in any other State which adopts this Act under clause (1) of Article 252 of the Constitution, on the date of such adoption; and any reference in this Act to the commencement of this Act shall, in relation to any State or Union territory, means the date on which this Act comes into force in such State or Union territory.

DATE OF ENFORCEMENT — Act came into force w.e.f. 4-2-1995 in the States of Goa, Himachal Pradesh and Maharashtra and in all the Union Territories *Vide* Noti. No. S.O. 80(E), dated 4-2-1995, published in the Gazette of India, Extra, Pt II, Section 3(ii), dated 4-2-1995.

2. Definitions — In Act, unless the context otherwise requires;

(*a*) "advertisement" includes any form of advertising whether to the public generally or to any section of the public or individually to selected persons;

(*b*) "Appropriate Authority" means the Appropriate Authority appointed under Section 13;

(c) "Authorisation Committee" means the committee constituted under clause (a) or clause (b) of sub-section (4) of Section 9;

(d) "brain-stem death" means the stage at which all functions of the brain-stem have permanently and irreversibly ceased and is so certified under sub-section (6) of Section 3;

(e) "deceased person" means a person in whom permanent disappearance of all evidence of life occurs, by reason of brain-stem death or in a cardio-pulmonary sense, at any time after live birth has taken place;

(f) "donor" means any person, not less than eighteen years of age, who voluntarily authorise the removal of any of his human organ for therapeutic purposes under sub-section (1) or sub-section (2) of Section 3;

(g) "hospital" includes a nursing home, clinic, medical centre, medical or teaching institution for therapeutic purpose and other like institution;

(h) "human organ" means any part of a human body consisting of a structured arrangement of tissues which, if wholly removed, cannot be replicated by the body;

(i) "near relative" means spouse, son, daughter, father, mother, brother or sister;

(j) "notification" means a notification published in the Official Gazette;

(k) "payment" means payment in money or money's worth but does not include any payment for defraying or reimbursing-

(i) the cost of removing, transporting or preserving the human organ to be supplied; or

(ii) any expenses or loss of earnings incurred by a person so far as reasonably and directly attributable to his supplying any human organ from his body;

(j) "prescribed' means prescribed by rules made under this Act;

(m) "recipient" means a person into whom any human organ is, or is proposed to be, transplanted;

(n) registered medical practitioner" means a medical practitioner who possesses any recognised medical qualification as defined in clause (h) of Section 2 of the Indian Medical Council Act, 1956 (102 of 1956), and who is enrolled on a State Medical Register as defined in clause (k) of that section;

(o) "therapeutic purposes" means systematic treatment of any disease or the measures to improve health according to any particular method or modality; and

(p) "transplantation" means the grafting of any human organ from any living person or deceased person to some other living person for therapeutic purposes.

II

AUTHORITY FOR THE REMOVAL OF HUMAN ORGANS

3. Authority for removal of human organs

(1) Any donor may, in such manner and subject to such conditions as may be prescribed, authorise the removal, before his death, of any human organ of his body for therapeutic purposes.

(2) If any donor had, in writing and in the presence of two or more witnesses (at least one of whom is a near relative of

such person), unequivocally authorised at any time before his death, the removal of any human organ of his body, after his death, for therapeutic purposes, the person lawfully in possession of the dead body of the donor shall, unless he has any reason to believe that the donor had subsequently revoked the authority aforesaid, grant to a registered medical practitioner all reasonable facilities for the removal for therapeutic purposes, of that human organ from the dead body of the donor.

(3) Where no such authority as is referred to in sub-section *(2)*, was made by any person before his death but no objection was also expressed by such person to any of his human organs being used after his death for therapeutic purpose, the person lawfully in possession of the dead body of such person may, unless he has reason to believe that nay near relative of the deceased person has objection to any of the deceased person's human organs being used for therapeutic purposes, authorise the removal of any human organ of the deceased person for its use for therapeutic purposes.

(4) The authority given under sub-section *(1)* or sub-section *(2)* or, as the case may be, sub-section *(3)* shall be sufficient warrant for the removal, for therapeutic purposes, of the human organ; but no such removal shall be made by any person other than the registered medical practitioner.

(5) Where any human organ is to be removed from the body of a deceased person, the registered medical practitioner shall satisfy himself before such removal, by a personal examination of the body from which any human organ is to be removed, that life is extinct in such body or, where it appears to be a case of brain-stem death, that such death has been certified under sub-section (6).

(6) Where any human organ is to be removed from the body of a person in the event of his brain-stem death, no such removal shall be undertaken unless such death is certified, in

such from and in such manner and on satisfaction of such conditions and requirements as may be prescribed, by a Board of medical experts consisting of the following, namely :-

(i) the registered medical practitioner in charge of the hospital in which brain-stem death has occurred;

(ii) an independent registered medical practitioner, being a specialist to be nominated by the registered medical practitioner specified in clause *(i)*, from the panel of names approved by the Appropriate Authority;

(iii) a neurologist or a neurosurge on to be nominated by the registered medical practitioner specified in clause (i), from the panel of names approved by the Appropriate Authority; and

(iv) the registered medical practitioner treating the person whose brain-stem death has occurred.

(7) Notwithstanding any think contained in sub-section(3) where brain-stem death of any person, less than eighteen years of age, occurs and is certified under sub-section (6), any of the parents of the deceased person may give authority, in such form and in such manner as may be prescribed, for the removal of any human organ from the body of the deceased person.

4. Removal of human organs not to be authorised in certain case

(1) No facilities shall be granted under sub-section (2) of Section 3 and no authority shall be given under sub-section (3) of that section for the removal of any human organ from the body of a deceased person if the person, required to grant such facilities or empowered to given such authority, has reason to believe that an inquest may be required to be held in relation to such body in pursuance of the provisions of any law for the time being in force.

(2) No authority for the removal of any human organ from the body of a deceased person shall be given by a person to whom such body has been entrusted solely for the purpose of interment, cremation or other disposal.

5. Authority for removal of human organs in case of unclaimed bodies in hospital or prison

(1) In the case of a dead body lying in a hospital or prison and not claimed by any of the near relatives of the deceased person with forty-eight hours from the time of the death of the concerned person, the authority for the removal of any human organ from the dead body which so remains unclaimed may be given, in the prescribed control of the hospital or prison, or by an employee of such hospital or prison authorised in this behalf by the person in charge of the management or control thereof.

(2) No authority shall be given under sub-section (1) if the person empowered to give such authority has reason to believe that any near relative of the deceased person is likely to claim the dead body even though such near relative has not come forward to claim the body of the deceased person within the time specified in sub-section (1).

6. Authority for removal of human organs from bodies sent for postmortem examination for medico-legal or pathological purposes

Where the body of a person has been sent for postmortem examination -

(a) for medico-legal purposes by reason of the death of such person having been caused by accident or any other unnatural cause; or

(b) for pathological purposes, the person competent

under this Act to give authority for the removal of any human organ from such dead body may, if he has reason to believe that such human organ will not be required for the purpose for which such body has been sent for postmortem examination, authorise the removal, for therapeutic purposes, of that human organ of the deceased person provided that he is satisfied that the deceased person, had not expressed, before his death, any objection to any of his human organs being used, for theapeutic purposes after his death or, where he had granted an authority for the use of any of his human organs for therapeutic purposes after his death, such authority had not been revoked by him before his death.

7. Preservation of human organs

After the removal of any human organ from the body of any person the registered medical practitioner shall take such steps for the preservation of the human organ so removed as may be prescribed.

8. Savings

(1) Nothing in the foregoing provisions of this Act shall be construed as rendering unlawful any dealing with the body or with any part of the body of a deceased person if such dealing would have been lawful if this Act had not been passed.

(2) Neither the grant of any facility or authority for the removal of any human organ from the body of a deceased person in accordance with the provisions of this Act nor the removal of any human organ from the body of a deceased person in pursuance of such authority shall be deemed to be an offence punishable under Section 297 of the Indian Penal Code (45 of 1860).

9. Restrictions on removal and transplantation of human organs

(1) Save as otherwise provided in sub-section (3), no

human organ removed from the body of a donor before his death shall be transplanted into a recipient unless the donor is a near relative of the recipient.

(2) Where any donor authorises the removal of any of his human organs after his death under sub-section (2) or Section 3 or any person competent or empowered to give authority for the removal, the human organ may be removed any transplanted into the body of any recipient who may be in need of such human organ.

(3) If any donor authorises the removal of any of his human organs before his death under sub-section (1) of Section 3 for transplantation into the body of such recipient not being a near relative as is specified by the donor by reason of affection or attachment towards the recipient or for any other special reasons, such human organ shall not be removed and transplanted without the prior approval of the Authorisation Committee.

(4) *(a)* The Central Government shall constitute, by notification, one or more Authorisation Committees consisting of such members as may be nominated by the Central Government on such terms and conditions as may be specified in the notification for each of the Union territories for the purposes of this section.

(b) The State Government shall constitute, by notification, one or more Authorisation Committee consisting of such members as may be nominated by the State Government on such terms and conditions as may be specified in the notification for the purposes of this section.

(5) On an application jointly made in such from and in such manner as may be prescribed, by the donor and the recipient, the Authorisation Committee shall, after holding as inquiry and after satisfying itself that the applicants have

complied with all the requirements of this Act and the rules made thereunder, grant to the applicants approval for the removal and transplantation of the human organ.

(6) If, after the inquiry and after giving an opportunity to the applicants of being heard, the Authorisation Committee is satisfied that the applicants have not complied with the requirements of this Act and the rules made thereunder, it shall for reasons to be recorded in writing, reject the application for approval.

III
REGULATION OF HOSPITALS

10. Regulation of hospitals conducting the removal, storage or transplantation of human organs

(1) On and from the commencement of the Act,—

(a) no hospital, unless registered under this Act, shall conduct, or associate with, or help in, the removal, storage or transplantation of any human organ;

(b) no medical practitioner or any other person shall conduct, or cause to be conducted, or aid in conducting by himself or through any other person, any activity relating to the removal, storage or transplantation of any human organ at a place other than a place registered under this Act; and

(c) no place including a hospital registered under sub-section (1) of Section 15 shall be used or cause to be used by any person for the removal, storage or transplantation of any human organ except for therapeutic purposes.

(2) Notwithstanding anything contained in sub-section (1),

the eyes or the ears may be removed at any place from the dead body of any donor, for therapeutic purposes, by a registered medical practitioner.

Explanation - For the purposes of this sub-section, "ears" includes ear drums and ear bones.

11. Prohibition of removal or transplantation of human organs for any purpose other than therapeutic purposes

No donor and no person empowered to give authority for the removal of any human organ shall authorise the removal of any human organ for any purpose other than therapeutic purposes.

12. Explaining effects, etc., to donor and recipient

No registered medical practitioner shall undertake the removal or transplantation of any human organ unless he had explained, in such manner as may be prescribed, all possible effect, complications and hazards connected with the removal and transplantation to the donor and the recipient respectively.

IV

APPROPRIATE AUTHORITY

13. Appropriate Authority

(1) The Central Government shall appoint, by notification, one or more officers as Appropriate Authorities for each of the Union territories for the purposes of this Act.

(2) The State Government shall appoint, by notification, one or more officers as Appropriate Authorities for the purposes of this Act.

(3) The Appropriate Authority shall perform the following functions, namely.:-

(i) to grant registration under sub-section (1) of

Section 15 or renew registration under sub-section (3) of that section;

(ii) to suspend or cancel registration under sub-section (2) of Section 16;

(iii) to enforce such standards, as may be prescribed, for hospitals engaged in the removal, storage of transplantation of any human organ;

(iv) to investigate any complaint of breach of any of the provisions of this Act or any of the rules made thereunder and take appropriate action;

(v) to inspect hospitals periodically for examination of the quality of transplantation and the follow-up medical care to persons who have undergone transplantation and persons from whom organs are removed; and

(vi) to undertake such other measures as may be prescribed.

V

REGISTRATION OF HOSPITALS

14. Registration of hospitals engaged in removal, storage or transplantation of human organs

(1) No hospital shall commence any activity relating to the removal, storage or transplantation of any human organ for therapeutic purposes after the commencement of this Act unless such hospital is duly registered under this Act :

Provided that every hospital engaged, either partly or exclusively, in any activity relating to the removal, storage or transplantation of any human organ for therapeutic purposes immediately before the commencement of this Act, shall apply for registration within sixty days from the date of such commencement :

Provided further that every hospital engaged in any activity relating to the removal, storage or transplantation of any human organ shall cease to engage in any such activity on the expiry of three months from the date of commencement of this Act unless such hospital has applied for registration and is so registered or till such application is disposed of, whichever is earlier.

(2) Every application for registration under sub-section (1) shall be made to the Appropriate Authority in such form and in such manner and shall be accompanied by such fees as may be prescribed.

(3) No hospital shall be registered under this Act unless the Appropriate Authority is satisfied that such hospital is in a position to provide such specialised services and facilities, possess such skilled manpower and equipments and maintain such standards as may be prescribed.

15. Certificate of registration

(1) The Appropriate Authority shall, after holding an inquiry and after satisfying itself that the applicant has complied with all the requirements of this Act and the rules made thereunder, grant to the hospital a certificate of registration in such form, for such period and subject to such conditions as may be prescribed.

(2) If, after the inquiry and after giving an opportunity to the applicant of being heard, the Appropriate Authority is satisfied that the applicant has not complied with requirements of this Act and the rules made thereunder, it shall, for reasons to be recorded in writing, reject the application for registration.

(3) Every certificate of registration shall be renewed in such manner and on payment of such fees as may be prescribed.

16. Suspension or cancellation of registration

(1) The Appropriate Authority may, suo moto or on complaint, issue a notice to any hospital to show cause why its registration under this Act should not be suspended or cancelled for the reasons mentioned in the notice.

(2) If, after giving a reasonable opportunity of being heard to the hospital, the Appropriate Authority is satisfied that there has been a breach of any of the provisions of this Act or the rules made thereunder, it may, without prejudice to any criminal action that it may take against such hospital, suspend its registration for such period as it may think fit or cancel its registration :

Provided that where the Appropriate Authority is of the opinion that it is necessary or expedient so to do in the public interest, it may, for reasons to be recorded in writing, suspend the registration of any hospital without issuing any notice.

17. Appeals

Any person aggrieved by an order of the Authorisation Committee rejecting an application for approval under sub-section (6) of Section 9, or any hospital aggrieved by an order of the Appropriate Authority rejecting an application for registration under sub-section (2) of Section 15 or an order of suspension or cancellation of registration under sub-section (2) of Section 16, may, within thirty days from the date of the receipt of the order, prefer an appeal, in such manner as may be prescribed, against such order to -

(i) the Central Government where the appeal is against the order of the Authorisation Committee constituted under clause (a) of sub-section (4) of Section 9 or against the order of the Appropriate Authority appointed under sub-section (1) of Section 13; or

(ii) the State Government, where the appeal is against the order of the Authorisation Committee constituted under clause (b) of sub-section (4) of Section 9 or against the order of the Appropriate Authority appointed under sub-section (2) of Section 13.

VI

OFFENCES AND PENALTIES

18. Punishment for removal of human organ without authority

(1) Any person who renders his services to or at any hospital and who, for purposes of transplantation, conducts, associates with, or helps in any manner in, the removal of any human organ without authority, shall be punishable with imprisonment for a term which may extend to five years and with fine which may extend to ten thousand rupees.

(2) Where any person convicted under sub-section (1) is a registered medical practitioner, his name shall be reported by the Appropriate Authority to the respective State Medical Council for taking necessary action including the removal of his name from the register of the Council for a period of two years for the first offence and permanently for the subsequent offence.

19. Punishment for commercial dealings in human organs —

Whoever

(a) makes or receives any payment for the supply of, or for an offer to supply, any human organ;

(b) seeks to find a person willing to supply for payment any human organ;

(c) offers to supply any human organ for payment;

(d) initiates or negotiates any arrangement involving the making of any payment for the supply of, or for an offer of supply, any human organ;

(e) takes part in the management or control of a body of persons, whether a society, firm or company, whose activities consist of or include the initiation or negotiation of any arrangement referred to in clause (d); or

(f) publishes or distributes or causes to be published or distributed any advertisement, -

(a) inviting persons to supply for payment of any human organ;

(b) offering to supply any human organ for payment; or

(c) indicating that the advertiser is willing to initiate or negotiate any arrangement referred to in clause (d), shall be punishable with imprisonment for a term which shall not be less than two years but which may extend to seven years and shall be liable to fine which shall not be less than ten thousand rupees but may extend to twenty thousand rupees :

Provided that the court may, for any adequate and special reason to be mentioned in the judgment, impose a sentence of imprisonment for a term of less than two years and a fine less than ten thousand rupees :

20. Punishment for contravention of any other provision of this Act

Whoever contravenes any provision of this Act or any rule made, or any condition of the registration granted, thereunder for which no punishment is separately provided in this Act, shall be punishable with imprisonment for a term which may extend to three years or with fine which may extend to five thousand rupees.

21. Offences by companies

(1) Where any offence, punishable under this Act, has been committed by a company, every person who, at the time the offence was committed was in charge of, and was responsible to, the company for the conduct of the business of the company, as well as the company, shall be deemed to be guilty of the offence and shall be liable to be proceeded against and published accordingly :

Provided that nothing contained in this sub-section shall render any such person liable to any punishment, if he proves that the offence was committed without his knowledge or that he had exercised all due diligence to prevent the commission of such offence.

(2) Notwithstanding anything contained in sub-section (1), where any offence punishable under this Act has been committed by a company and it is proved that the offence has been committed with the consent or connivance of, or is attributable to any neglect on the part of, any director, manager, secretary or other officer of the company, such director, manager, secretary or other officer shall also be deemed to be guilty of that offence and shall be liable to be proceeded against and punished accordingly.

Explanation - For the purposes of this section, -

(a) "company" means any body corporate and includes a firm or other association of individuals; and

(b) "director", in relation to a firm, means a partner in the firm.

NOTES

Offence by Company - The Company cannot be prosecuted for offences involving mean rea and/or involving compulsory punishment of imprisonment. *A.K. Khosla v. T.S.*

Venkatesan, 1992 Cri LJ 448 (Cal) [*Champa Agency v. R. Chowdhury,* 1974 CHN 400; *Sunil Chandra v. Krishna Chandra,* AIR 1949 Cal 689; *Machine India Ltd. v. State,* (1987) 1 CHN 359; *Kusum v. S.K. Sinha,* (1980) 2 CHN 326; *East India Jute and Hessian Exchange Ltd. v. Amulya Krishna Mondal,* 1989 C CrLR 171, followed. *MCD v. J.B. Bottling Co.,* 1975 Cri LJ 1148 (Del FB) dissented from].

Municipal Corporation can be prosecuted for offences which are only punishable with fine. Imprisonment of Municipal Corporation is out of question. *Girdharilal v. Lalchand,* AIR 1970 Raj 145: 1970 Cri LJ 987.

A company or body corporate is not a "person" within the meaning of Art. 20(3) of the Constitution. *Godrej Soap Co. Ltd. v. State,* 1991 Cri LJ 828 (Cal).

The accused had a domicile of origin in the district of Multan and had to be assigned Pakistani domicile on partition of India. He committed an offence in Pakistan. He cannot be tried for the offence by a Criminal Court of India after his migration of India on his acquisition of the status of a citizen of India. *Central Bank of India Ltd. v. RAm Narain,* AIR 1955 SC 36: 1955 Cri LJ 152.

22. Cognizance of offences

(1) No court shall take cognizance of an offence under this Act except on a complaint made by —

(a) the Appropriate Authority concerned, or any officer authorised in this behalf by the Central Government or the State Government or, as the case may be, the Appropriate Authority; or

(b) a person who has given notice of not less than sixty days, in such manner as may be prescribed, to the Appropriate Authority concerned, of the alleged offence and of his intention to make a complaint to the court.

(2) No court other than that of a Metropolitan Magistrate of a Judicial Magistrate of the first class shall try any offence punishable under this Act.

(3) Where a complaint has been made under clause (b) of sub-section (1), the court may, on demand by such person, direct the Appropriate Authority to make available copies of the relevant records in its possession to such person.